DD801
O35
W47

THE
ODER - NEISSE PROBLEM

Towards Fair Play in Central Europe

NOV 16 1970

155448

Author: Friedrich von Wilpert

Edition Atlantic-Forum
Bonn — Brussels — New York
1964

Copyright by Edition Atlantic-Forum 1964

TABLE OF CONTENTS

Chapter 10:

AN ISSUE THAT CONCERNS THE WORLD

FOREWORD

If a group of informed and open-minded Germans were to sit down for a discussion with a group of like-minded Poles, the Germans might well open the discussion, for their side, with some such message as this.

*

Four times your Polish land has been partitioned. You Poles, perhaps more than any other people in the world, know what men will endure, how long they will wait, to what lengths they will go, to keep alive the concept of homeland.

As we have told the Jewish people, we are keenly aware that there can be no complete atonement for such human suffering as was inflicted in the years 1939—1945. We have endeavored continuously, ever since the creation of the Federal Republic, to make what moral and tangible restitution we could to the Jewish people and their survivors. We are more than ready, we are eager, to make the same overtures to the people of Poland, our nearest Eastern neighbors.

We hope that one day a government speaking for the Polish people will accept our readiness to offer restitution in the spirit in which it is meant: as both a tangible payment and the only way in which we can say to you, our neighbors: "What happened between us was not our wish. Let us build our future together in peace."

We hope that through your representatives you will meet with us, as soon as you are free to do so. At that time, let us talk over both restitution and all other questions that may divide us.

Where the frontiers between Poland and Germany are concerned, let us work out a settlement by which, so far as we and you can humanly devise, no single person will lose. In the so-called Oder-Neisse area in particular, let us discuss citizenship rights, majority and minority freedoms, freedom of faith and language and residence. Here in Central Europe, let us set an example by guaranteeing each other these and all the other freedoms that both our peoples have lost so often in recent history, and cherish the more.

We also make this offer in the name of the German people in the Soviet Zone who cannot yet speak for themselves.

But in offering to make restitution and to clear up other problems between us, we ask you not to demand of us what you would not wish others to ask of you. Do not ask us to pay by giving away something that is not ours to give away: a part of our homeland.

It is our homeland, too, you may reply. Many of our people have been settled in what you call your Eastern Territories. Since 1945, the regime that rules us has called the area our Western Territories. Let us discuss that situation, too, when both our peoples are free to negotiate as honorable and equal partners. There is no need for any single Pole or any single German to suffer from a fair and negotiated settlement of the lands that lie between us.

No boundary need be a division between two peoples who through most of their history have been good neighbors, whenever their overlords permitted them to be so. The free, democratic Germany that has emerged since 1949 has won the trust of its neighbors to the West. Border settlements have been reached. Traditional enmities have been replaced by cooperation. Mutual prosperity has grown. What has been achieved in the West can be achieved, when the time comes, in the East.

May the unilateral actions, the enforced arrangements that have troubled your people and ours since 1945 one day be replaced by a fair, negotiated settlement. Then no one will be the poorer. On the contrary, the people of Poland, the people of Germany, the people of Europe will be the richer.

INTRODUCTION

This book is dedicated to the proposition that two wrongs can never make a right.

The immediate wrongs involved are:

* *Adolf Hitler's attack on Poland in 1939,* an invasion that touched off world war and brought untold suffering to Poles, Germans, and peoples of many other nations;

* *Communism's aggression against Europe since 1945,* an aggression that is no more based on the consent of the peoples of the East Bloc than was the 1939 action by the Hitler dictatorship the wish of the German people.

This book rejects both wrongs, and proposes a new start based on fair play between two neighbors in Central Europe: Poland and Germany.

The thesis propounded in the following pages is not simply a German thesis, although it appears in a book published in the Federal Republic of Germany — and published in the interests, too, of those 16 million Germans of the Soviet Zone who cannot yet speak for themselves. What appears here is basically the thesis of the victorious Allies of 1945. They put it in writing in the Potsdam Agreement: *The future of Germany's borders in Central Europe can be settled only in a peace treaty concluded with representatives of the whole German people.*

It was not a German, but a Soviet Russian, who said "Peace is indivisible." If there is to be world peace, there must be peace in Europe. If there is to be self-determination elsewhere in the world, there must be self-determination for Germans and their neighbors in Central Europe.

Such a future in freedom cannot be based on the postwar hatreds and fears of 1945, on the unilateral acts of aggression and greed that grew out of the provisional wartime settlements. From Europe armed against itself must come Europe the continent of good neighbors. Right must one day emerge from a tangle of past wrongs.

The chain of errors must be broken. History questions the Polish seizure of territory from the Soviet Union in 1921. Wrong indeed was Hitler's and Stalin's partition of Poland in 1939. The seizure by a Polish government (never freely elected by the Polish people) in the year since 1945 of lands that have been German for centuries, lands that were only to be "provisionally administered" by the Polish until a peace settlement — that too was wrong. If right is to triumph, wrong must have a stop.

In the West, the German people, free of a war-minded dictatorship, represented by a democratically elected German government, ashamed of the past under Hitler and intent on building a future on principles of humanity, have won the trust of their Western neighbors. In the short years since the birth of the Federal Republic in 1949, Germany and its western neighbors have in fact become one Europe. The day will come when there will be a similarly peaceful, similarly democratic government representing Germany as a whole. That government will deserve the trust of its neighbors in the East.

Meanwhile, no settlements must be made that perpetuate the tensions, that lengthen the chain of historical wrongs in Central Europe. The way must be left open for negotiation one day — as soon as possible — on a solution that will keep the peace in Central Europe for all future generations.

This book looks forward to such a settlement between a free Germany and Poland. In looking ahead, it looks back, to explore the problem of the Oder-Neisse area, of Germany's traditional Eastern Territories. It proposes no unilateral settlement of national boundaries by either Poland or Germany. Its only demand is for peaceful negotiations. For only an honest settlement will serve the real, long-range interests of both Poles and Germans. Only fair play will advance the cause of peace in Europe, and therefore in the world.

Chapter 1:

THE PROBLEM

The problem discussed in this book is a German problem, a Polish problem, a European problem and a world problem.

The German Problem

Stated in German terms, the situation is this:

Nearly ten million Germans have been driven from their homeland east of the Oder and western Neisse rivers, an area that has been German for centuries; and they, their children and their countrymen are being prevented from returning;

One-fourth of the total area of Germany is under Polish administration;

A people that has done its best since 1945 to make a fresh start from its and Europe's past has been forced for 19 years to submit to a situation in central Europe that is building up new tensions for the future;

A nation the free part of which has earned the trust of the free world, that consistently champions self-determination for others, is itself partitioned and unfree.

The Polish Problem

Stated in Polish terms, the situation is this:

A regime not chosen by the Polish people in free elections has tried, at Soviet Communist urging, to absorb into Poland a territory that for centuries has belonged to Poland's neighbor;

A people proud of its traditional affiliation with the West has seen its rulers acquiesce in Soviet violation of agreements that Poland's own champions — Great Britain, the United States, France — solemnly concluded with the Soviet Union in 1945;

A nation that has itself suffered long under partition is helping to perpetuate the partition of a neighbor nation.

The European Problem

Stated in European terms, the situation is this:

A continent is being partitioned along lines that run through Germany, that continent's geographical centre;

A European family of nations that have achieved harmonious and prosperous relations in the west are being prevented arbitrarily from fostering similar friendly relations in the east;

Europe, which geography and modern technology have combined to make one, is split in two by a line its people have not drawn;

That segment of the Iron Curtain called the Oder-Neisse Line, together with the segment that separates Soviet-controlled Germany from free Germany, constitute a line of demarcation between Europe's free and unfree peoples.

The World Problem

To summarize from an international viewpoint:

There is tension in partitioned Germany, and a source of tension in the heart of Europe is a threat to peoples everywhere;

The German-Polish situation violates principles — freedom, self-determination, the right to a homeland — that the United Nations are struggling to establish and uphold in Africa and Asia;

As everywhere else, principles of fair play ultimately must win in Europe, for the world has learned that "peace is indivisible."

12

The Oder-Neisse Situation as Part of the Germany Problem

Perhaps because the human mind prefers to focus on one problem at a time, it is tempting to think of the dramatic and highly tangible situation in Berlin as constituting the whole of the east-west problem in Germany and Europe. But actually, as statesmen have long recognized, Berlin is an integral part rather than the whole of the German problem. There are three parts to the German question:

1. The question of Berlin: It is divided at this writing into French, British and American Sectors — in which the people hold free elections — and a Soviet Sector, in which they do not.

2. The question of the Soviet Zone of Germany: Its people are not free to join their countrymen in the Federal Republic of Germany, and, like the people of East Berlin, they have not had a free election since the Soviet occupation government took over in 1945.

3. The question of the Eastern Territories along the Oder and the Neisse rivers: By agreement of the occupation powers in 1945, these areas were assigned to Polish *administration* "pending conclusion of a peace treaty with the whole of Germany."

As for Berlin, the occupation powers pledged that it would remain under Four-Power control. Since that time, freedom has been extinguished in the Soviet Sector of the city, East Berlin. Unless West Berlin is defended until all Berlin can become the capital of a reunited Germany, the free world will have surrendered one of its most important beach-heads of liberty.

As for Central Germany or the Soviet Zone, the occupation powers in 1945 contemplated Germany's reunification after all-German elections. The Western Allies repeated that commitment in the London agreement of 1954. Unless that pledge is kept, the free world will have surrendered to the East Bloc immense lands and resources — plus more than 17,000,000 Central Germans who live for the day of reunion with their West German countrymen in freedom from fear. That pledge must be kept for an even more important reason: To end the partition of the world, the

13

partition of Europe must be ended. To end the partition of Europe, the partition of Germany must be ended.

As for the German Eastern Territories, the occupation powers, including the Soviet Union, declared that the status of the Oder-Neisse area would be kept open pending a German peace treaty. Unless that pledge is kept, the free world will have rewarded a unilateral act of annexation; will have made a present to the Communist Bloc of immense lands and resources, without even negotiating; and will have provided Europe with a heritage of tension for generations to come.

The Geography of Divided Germany

"The problem of a divided world", as a member of the U. S. House of Representatives has put it *, "is largely the problem of a divided Europe. The problem of a divided Europe is almost entirely the problem of a divided Germany."

This divided Germany is the Germany of 1937 before Hitler began his conquests. The territory now under the rule of a Communist puppet regime, styling itself "Government of the German Democratic Republic" ("DDR"), is often mistakenly referred to as East Germany. In reality it is but the central part or middle Germany, while East Germany comprises the part east of the rivers Oder and the western Neisse — roughly speaking, the provinces of East Prussia, Pomerania, Silesia and part of Brandenburg.

The Oder-Neisse Line, which delineates the German Eastern Territories occupied by Poland since 1945, is 456 kilometres (about 275 miles) long. Beginning on the Baltic at Swinemünde, it stretches

---

* The late Rep. B. Carroll Reece of Tennessee. For a comprehensive summary of the economic, historical, legal and political aspects of the Oder-Neisse problem, see his remarks in the Congressional Record, House, 85th Congress, 1st Session, Vol. 103, No. 82, May 16, 1957, pp. 6346—6361. Also available from U.S. Government Printing Office, Washington, 1957, No. 427029—62503, as "Speech of Hon. B. Carroll Reece of Tennessee in the House of Representatives", Thursday, May 16, 1957.

14

southward from Stettin to the Oder, cuts in two, among others, the cities of Frankfurt-on-the-Oder, Guben and Görlitz, follows the western Neisse (Lausitzer Neisse) and ends at Zittau on the Czechoslovakian border. The area comprises 114,291 square kilometres — twice the area of Switzerland — of which 102,985 square kilometres is under Polish administration and the rest was assigned by the Potsdam Agreement to the Soviet Union.

The Oder-Neisse Problem:
The German Domestic Aspect

Since 1945, a great deal of attention has been paid to the question of establishing the roots of genuine democracy in Germany. A great deal of attention has been paid also — and sometimes of course purely for reasons of political opportunism — to the question of whether the German people might resort to force to end their present partition. In the years since 1945, the west Germans have won the trust and respect of the non-Communist world; and the democracy of the Federal Republic of Germany can afford to stand on its record. Over those same years, the German people have pledged their honor to uphold their right of a homeland only through peaceful means.

But history teaches that the continued failure of a policy of reason and moderation courts the danger that such a policy may become devalued even in the eyes of those practicing it. This danger hardly exists in West Germany today, where the population is committed to a democratic form of government. But Germany remains partitioned into free western Germany, Soviet-occupied central Germany and Polish-occupied eastern Germany. If totalitarianism is allowed to perpetuate this situation — after a war that was fought to defeat a totalitarian regime — what will be the faith and credit of democracy in central Europe? If Communist regimes succeed in dictating a major frontier in central Europe against the will of the people affected, how can the free peoples assure the unfree central Germans, the unfree eastern Europeans, or for that matter the unfree populations elsewhere in the world that democracy is worth waiting for?

In the long run, moreover, there is also the attitude of the west German public to take into account. Ever since 1949, when the Federal Republic was born, the west German electorate has supported only the moderate, democratic political parties. Those parties have pledged that (1) there will be a reunified Germany and (2) Germany's eastern frontiers will be negotiated at a peace conference. Overwhelmingly, the west German electorate has trusted these pledges. In turn, the democratic political parties have trusted the pledges made repeatedly by Germany's allies — notably in the London agreement of 1954 — to support the goals of (1) reunification and (2) negotiation of the eastern frontiers.

Now suppose these pledges are abandoned, either by German statesmen, or by Germany's allies, or by world public opinion. Suppose that by some default of democratic will and purpose Germany is allowed indefinitely to remain split into three parts: her central part and her eastern part under two different although related totalitarian regimes. If this situation is allowed to continue, who can predict the attitude of future generations of west Germans? Who can say what Germans of the future will think of a democratic and moderate policy that has failed even to unite their own homeland?

On the other hand, a settlement of the Oder-Neisse question that shows consideration for the rights of all affected peoples would be a big forward step. It would contribute immensely toward stabilizing the foundations of democratic faith within Germany and in Europe — today and for unborn generations.

The Foreign-Policy Aspect

Even the present uneasy balance in the world is preferable to war. The principal nations charged with maintaining that balance on the side of the free world are the members of the North Atlantic Alliance. The Federal Republic of Germany is a member of NATO

16

— and the one nation in the world to have completely merged her armed forces with those of an international organization.

The Western allies of the Federal Republic of Germany have asserted (as they and the Soviet Union asserted at the Potsdam Conference of 1945) that they consider the Oder-Neisse Line a provisional line of demarcation. As Germany depends upon her allies for the maintenance of her rights, this assurance has immense psychological importance.

If the Federal Republic of Germany were no longer able to be certain of the support of her allies in the Oder-Neisse question, then an important pillar of her foreign policy, which is grounded on trust in the West, would be shaken.

To state this potential danger is no more than to reflect a reality of democracy: that public opinion governs a nation's policy. German public opinion is overwhelmingly with the West. Only a failure of the West to continue to treat Germany as a partner with the same rights of nationhood that the other Western nations take to be self-evident could weaken that partnership. Fortunately for the security of both non-aligned and Western nations, it is inconceivable that there will be any such disruption of the ties that bind the North Atlantic community of peoples.

The Aspect of Distribution of Population

Even in the years before 1945, the population density of the Oder-Neisse territories was not especially great. The rich and fertile area was capable in the long run of supporting more people than the 12 million Germans who lived there. Today about 6 to 7 million Poles live there — a population that does not begin to be sufficient to exploit the area's natural resources, and, moreover, a population that has not been able to grow even after the application by the Polish government of an energetic resettlement policy.

The situation described above is of course an opportunity for good neighbors to work out a settlement policy to their mutual benefit. (Such a policy is mentioned as one of several possibilities for an Oder-Neisse agreement, in Chapter 9 of this book.)

Meanwhile, the population imbalance that has resulted from the arbitrary rearrangement of borders in central Europe is striking. The problem has been emphasized, of course, by the forced movement westward of expellees from the Eastern Territories and by the flight of refugees from the Soviet Zone of Germany. The existing imbalance is shown at a glance by the following comparison:

In the Eastern Territories (the Oder-Neisse area that is now being occupied by Poland), there are, at most, an estimated 83 persons per square kilometre;

In central Germany (the Soviet Zone or "German Democratic Republic") there are 160 persons per square kilometre;

In West Germany (the Federal Republic) there are 222 persons per square kilometre.

The Economic Aspect

Seen economically, too, there is needless imbalance in central Europe. To take for a moment only the case of Germany alone, the arbitrary changes in frontiers since 1945 have completely upset her traditional domestic economic patterns.

In these days of regional and world economic co-operation, a distorted economic structure in any one nation can, especially in times of economic stress, be a strain on the economies of other nations. Moreover, aid to the developing countries depends on the most efficient functioning of the older industrialized economies.

In order to get an idea what the loss of the German Eastern Territories means to the German (and therefore the international) economy, one should consider that:

The German areas east of the Oder-Neisse line comprise 25 percent, or one-fourth, of the workable agricultural land of all Germany;

18

The area supplied more than half of Germany's production of grain before the second world war. Its grain production equaled that of Australia, its potato production that of France, its butterfat production that of Denmark;

The area supplied almost 95 percent of Germany's copper, 55 percent of its zinc and about 65 percent of its domestic resources of potash;

Polish occupation of the Oder-Neisse area has also deprived Germany of traditional sources of other products ranging from textiles to machinery.

Incidentally, the Communist argument that the Oder-Neisse areas were owned by a small "upper crust" of Prussian Junkers is false. Instead, in Pomerania 65 percent, in East Prussia 69 percent and in Silesia 74 percent of the agricultural land was in the hands of farmers whose individual holdings did not exceed 250 acres.

This look at how things were is by no means to suggest that there should ever again be a return to attempts at economic nationalism or self-sufficiency. On the contrary, the free peoples of the West are providing an example of what could also be achieved across borders, for the common good, if arbitrariness were to be replaced by fair settlements in central Europe.

Particularly in Western Europe, the phenomenal success of the Common Market has made possible higher levels of trade, along with an increased ability to help the developing nations. That achievement is an example of what can take place in the East once the artificial situation existing between Germany and Poland has been corrected, and once manpower and goods can move without unnecessary restrictions.

The Historical Aspect

Areas that have been part of one particular country and one culture for more than 700 years without interruption are part and parcel of that nation. This (see Chapter 3) is the case with the Oder-Neisse area.

Territorial demands by others, alleging a "possession" that lies still further back in time, are both dubious on their face and unrealistic in that they fail to recognize the fact of organic "belonging" that has developed through 700 years of historical evolution.

The Oder-Neisse territories were absorbed into the German cultural sphere over a period extending from the 13th to the 15th centuries. Long before there was a Russian empire and before America was discovered, the border between this region and Poland was fixed. This border has since been unaltered, and *it is counted among the oldest borders in European history.*

There can be negotiations between neighbors about a given area, but there can be no unilateral decision about it. A people cannot simply renounce, even if they wish to do so, a part of their homeland that has played an integral role in their literature, their economy, their culture and their history.

The Legal Aspect

The Polish Communist claim to the Oder-Neisse territories is unfounded. It was largely manufactured in Moscow (see Chapter 5), and it corresponds neither to genuine Polish interests nor to international law. In the Potsdam Agreement, Poland received these areas only for administration. The final settlement was expressly reserved for a peace treaty with Germany. The Western powers have repeatedly reaffirmed this decision. It is denied, for shortsighted reasons of supposed political advantage, only within the Communist Bloc.

An "agreement" concluded by the regime ruling the Soviet-occupied zone of Germany (the so-called "German Democratic Republic" or "DDR") and the Communist regime in Poland has declared the Oder-Neisse Line to be the final "national border" (see Chapter 6). This "agreement" ignores the Four-Power agreement of Potsdam. Moreover, the totalitarian, Bolshevist regime that now has power in Central Germany was not chosen by the people it rules; it is not authorized to speak for the 17 million Germans within its sphere of domination, let alone for the 55 million Germans of the Federal Republic or for the whole of Germany. This "agreement" to recognize the Oder-Neisse Line, consequently, is of no weight whatsoever. That fact is confirmed by the Communist Bloc's unceasing and generally fruitless efforts to win other nations' "recognition" of the illegal boundary. This international recognition has not been forthcoming — for recognition of the Oder-Neisse Line as the German-Polish frontier would, under present circumstances, be a breach of international law.

As the Allies recognized, their military occupation of Germany did not effect a territorial change of title. According to international law, the "unconditional surrender" of Germany was a military surrender — not a subjugation or an annexation.

In fact, the German generals would not have had legal power of attorney to sign away any German territory. It is a generally accepted rule of international law that a military commander has no power to "agree to terms of a political nature or such as will take effect after the termination of hostilities."

The above-quoted rule is part of the Hague Convention of 1907, which the Soviet Government, for example, has expressly recognized and upon the enforcement of which it has repeatedly insisted. The subsequent political arrangement at Potsdam was expressly declared to be provisional — pending a treaty of peace which has yet to be concluded.

Moreover, the expulsion from their native homelands east of the Oder-Neisse Line of 10 million Germans — a population equal in size to the combined population of Sweden and Norway — is a violation of the principle of self-determination of peoples. It thus constitutes a violation of human rights, as also of present-day international law. The pressure of wartime under which the Western Allies were deceived by the Soviet Government and the Polish Communist regime as to the facts of the expulsion (Chapter 5) may be understandable; but the circumstances under which the expulsion occurred cannot make it legal.

The Ideological Aspect

Every concession to the Communist Bloc since the end of the second world war has led to new crises and new demands. Given the East-West tensions in Europe, there is no ground for the West to renounce an object of negotiation — the Oder-Neisse area of Germany — without a *comparable* return; and no ground whatsoever for making such a concession (1) without consulting the free German people as a whole and (2) even before serious East-West negotiations for a genuine, over-all peace settlement have begun.

Moreover, the question of where the borderline of Moscow's totalitarian brand of Communism is to be drawn cannot be a matter of indifference to the free peoples. After a reunification of Germany, the German-Polish border, wherever it is established, would also be the dividing line between the free and the non-free world.

Quite aside from the ultimate destiny of the presently unfree peoples of eastern Europe, both humanitarian and political considerations demand that no peaceful effort should be spared to roll back the sway of totalitarian Communism behind the *natural* western borders of Poland.

The Moral Aspect

The crimes that Hitler committed against the Polish people in the name of Germany impose on the German people the obligation of restitution. Germany recognizes this restitution as not only a tangible but also a moral debt. The Germans see the two-fold obligation as part of the task of restoring to the world a system of relationships based on justice.

The possibility that part of such restitution can consist of freely negotiated territorial arrangements is not being disputed. Nothing would be more in accord with the policy of the Federal Government of Germany than to call for tangible sacrifices by the German people for the Polish people.

But such sacrifices, if they are to be in the long-range interest of good international relationships, must be measured by the restraints of reason and of statesmanlike foresight.

Sacrifice of German territory under present circumstances would not be a contribution to world peace but rather a concession to a Communist Bloc policy that sees in a neighbor's readiness to yield only an opportunity to prepare demands for new concessions. "Two wrongs do not make a right," goes the old saying. The remedies for past wrongs in Europe's history can come only through international negotiation. In regard to the Oder-Neisse situation, only a free and united German people can negotiate the question of its eastern frontiers.

At present the Communist-ruled Germans who face the Communist-ruled Poles along the Oder-Neisse Line are not free to decide their domestic affairs, let alone to negotiate an issue of international boundaries. One day the liberal traditions of the Polish people — themselves so often in the past the victims of national partition — will be able to reassert themselves. One day the German people will be reunited. They will be more than ready to negotiate with a Polish government to reach an honorable settlement — on national lines, international lines, or a combination of both (see Chapter 9) — in central Europe.

Chapter 2:

WHY THERE *IS* NO "STATUS QUO"

"We are told that the division of our country is a 'reality' which has to be accepted. Of course it is a reality, but it is an unbearable one. An illness, too, is a reality, but no one would think of blaming someone who tries to protect himself from and to cure the disease. Injustice is also a reality, and yet we shall have to do all we can to remove it. But above all, if the division of our country is put forward as a reality, the will of the German people to restore its unity is a far stronger reality, for history has shown that the fundamental urge of a nation to fight for its unity and freedom is one of the mightiest powers of all".

German Chancellor Ludwig Erhard,
to parliament, October 18, 1963

"Why not leave things as they are?" ask many people of good will when confronted with the Oder-Neisse situation. "Isn't it better to maintain the status quo in central Europe than to change things? Isn't peace better than the risk of war?"

The true answer is that while there is no war in Europe, the present situation is so artificial that it is no foundation for peace. In this sense there is no "status quo". For a "status quo" implies some measure of stability; a situation that can be reasonably maintained; a point of rest. But the German-Polish situation is none of these things.

24

Both Poland and the part of Germany that fronts on the Oder-Neisse border are unfree lands today. Two peoples oppressed are separated by a line that neither has drawn. The Poles are ruled by a regime that dare not make a foreign-policy move independently of Moscow. The Germans of the Soviet Zone of Germany are ruled by a government that also is closely controlled by Moscow.

Neither the Poles to the east of the Oder-Neisse Line (most of those who live in the German Eastern Territories are there, incidentally, as a result of an artificial settlement policy sponsored by their Communist government) nor the Germans in the Soviet Zone just to the west of the line have known free and secret elections since the end of the second world war.

As for the border that presently divides these two unfree peoples — the Communist-controlled Poles and the Communist-controlled part of the German people — we shall be reminded in Chapter 5 that it is a provisional border. Those who drew it meant it to be provisional, and said so. By its nature, indeed, it has to be provisional — because the peoples whom it divides have not had a chance to choose it. Communist propaganda calls the Oder-Neisse Line a "peace frontier"; actually the line is maintained, in the last analysis, by the armed might of the Red Army and its satellite armies of the East Bloc.

This is not to say that the Germans or their allies would ever use force to correct the border. On the contrary, the North Atlantic Alliance is a defensive organization; and the armed forces of the Federal Republic of Germany are merged within NATO. Moreover, the Federal Government has repeatedly and specifically renounced the use of armed might in settling any territorial question, including that of the Polish-German frontier.

But all of Europe's history has shown that there is only continuing tension when solutions are imposed on peoples by force. Moreover, the history of our century indicates that there is no foundation for genuine peace as long as a people is denied the right of self-determination.

The Oder-Neisse Line has been imposed on the German people and on the Polish people. Many Poles feel uneasy about the moral and political aspects of a Polish occupation of German Eastern Territories (see Chapter 5, 6 and 7). As for the Germans, they cannot rewrite history even if with the best will in the world they were to try to do so: The Eastern Territories have been German for six centuries and longer (see Chapter 3). Moreover, they have been German not only through political sovereignty but also in a cultural and an economic sense. They are as much a part of German national consciousness as any comparable area would be part of the national consciousness of any other people (see comparison map facing page).

To this a person of good will who hopes against hope that there may be a "status quo" worth upholding in central Europe may say: "All that is true. But isn't it also true that there are no longer any Germans living in the Eastern Territories?" With important exceptions (see Chapter 6), that is so. But the very fact of the forcible expulsion of some ten million Germans from their homeland has created an open wound and an issue of all-German concern. It is an error widely entertained — but an error — to suppose that within Germany the Eastern Territories have only some lingering sentimental value for an aging generation of expellees. On the contrary (quite aside from the expellees' children, who have absorbed their parents' vivid memories of home) the enormity of the expulsion has tended to dramatize the problem of the Eastern Territories to the whole German people. Losing one-fourth of their nation has created an indelible impression on Germans who normally would have taken the existence of the lands beyond the Oder-Neisse for granted.

Public-opinion polls have indicated that the desire for reunification of western and central Germany has taken on a higher priority with the German public as the years roll on. Similarly, the wish has grown with every passing year for a settlement of the Eastern Territories problem.

While there is desire for fair play, this is not to say there is a spirit of "revenge" or "revisionism" in Germany. It was not the

Germans who tried after 1945 to revise the map of Europe, and they are not proposing to revise it. They protest, rather, the arbitrary revisionism that has been visited on the map of central Europe not by Germans but by Communist policy, unilaterally, without benefit of international consultation.

Yet the Oder-Neisse arrangement, according to its own sponsors, was meant to be only provisional pending a peace treaty. As Chapter 5 documents in more detail, what has happened in central Europe since 1945 was never the wish nor the intention of the Western Allies who were partners to the wartime and postwar agreements. The arrangement was not even submitted to the Polish people; they have yet to have a chance to express themselves through a democratically elected government. For that promise of 1945, too — democracy in Poland — has been broken by unilateral Communist decision.

This is why there is no true "status quo" in central Europe. There is only an uneasy state of affairs upheld by force of arms. It will not be corrected by force of arms. But it will be replaced one day, and the sooner the better for all the peoples of the world — replaced with an arrangement worked out by the free German people and representatives of the Polish people meeting at a peace conference.

Chapter 3:

POLISH-GERMAN RELATIONS
THROUGH THE CENTURIES

At the beginning of the first milennium after the birth of Christ, Germanic tribes settled in the area between the Baltic Sea and the Black Sea. These included above all the Goths, who came over from Scandinavia at about 150 A. D. and extended their realm during the next two centuries so that at the time of King Ermanrich they ruled the whole area between the two seas. Other tribes worthy of mention are the *Rugier*, the *Burgundians*, the *Langobards*, the *Vandals*, and — in the area of present-day Silesia — the *Silinger*.

When the empire of the Goths succumbed to the onrush of the Huns in the middle of the 4th century, the West Goths migrated to the lower Danube. The other Germanic tribes who were settled on the Dnieper, the Vistula and the Oder moved westward, and we encounter them again in Italy, France, Spain and even in North Africa. Into the areas they vacated there moved — also driven by pressure of the Mongols — several Baltic and Slavic tribes.

As early as the German era there was a lively commerce between the peoples on the Baltic Sea and the Mediterranean countries. Well-known in this connection is the so-called "Amber Road", which extends from the Amber Coast of the Baltic Sea up the Vistula, and at Breslau crosses over into the valley of the Oder to Carnuntum, near what is today Vienna.

After the Tribal Migrations

After the Germanic tribes moved away, we find inhabiting the Baltic area the *Esthonians* (who are related to the Finns), the *Liven* and the *Kuren*. Later these peoples give way to the Letts or Latvians, whose language, along with the Lithuanian tongue, is one of the oldest indo-Germanic languages.

In the present-day East Prussia settled the *Pruzzen*, who gave the country its name and are related to the Lithuanians. Farther west, in the areas to be known later as West Prussia and Pomerania, were residing the *Pomeranen* ("those who dwell on the sea") — thence the names Pomerelia and Pomerania — the German "Pommerellen" and "Pommern" and the Polish "Pomorze" — for the areas located south of the Baltic.

Along the middle Vistula to the Warthe, where the Kingdom of the East Goths had had its beginnings, there now settled the *Polanen* (Poljana = forest clearing; Poles = inhabitants of the fields), and, at the upper course of the Vistula, the *Wislanen*.

In the Silesian area, six additional Slavic tribes established themselves from 600 A. D. onward, among them the *Slesanen* from which Silesia later took its name. All these tribes led a life of their own, and recurrently engaged in bloody battles with one another. The momentarily stronger made the others pay tribute after the manner of a feudal arrangement.

The Middle Ages

At about the year 1000, the Christianization of the Slavs begins. The first bishoprics were Kolberg (for the Pomeranians), Breslau (for the Silesians), Cracow (for the Wislanen) and — as the only archbishopric — Gnesen (for the Poles).

In order to comprehend the eventful history of the peoples of these areas, one must bear in mind that in this region the rival claims and political interests of German, Polish and Czech sovereigns frequently crossed. The various rulers endeavored each to bring an area under his own domain, and to exact feudal tribute from the Slavic tribes. From the beginning, these rivalries were a basic element in the history of Poland.

How Did Poland Come Into Existence?

The Polish people can trace their ancestral line back to the *Polanes*, who settled in the Warthe-Netze area and at the middle Vistula; and to the *Wislanen*, who settled along the Vistula's upper reaches. The 10th century brings the first mention of a Polish duke: In the year 963, we find this Duke Mieszko giving his oath of allegiance to the German Margrave Gero. The oldest capital of Poland was Gnesen, replaced by Cracow only in the 14th century. Far later, the capital of the Polish state was moved to Warsaw.

Mieszko proceeded to conquer Silesia, which was in Bohemian (Czech) possession. His son Bolesław Chrobry (the Brave) extended the kingdom on all sides by victorious campaigns. He conquered Lasatia, Pomerania, Moravia, Slovakia, and he pushed forward to the southeast, far into the part of Russia known now as the Ukraine. After taking Kiev, he had himself crowned king.

Since that time there has been a kingdom of Poland. Under Bolesław Chrobry's successors the major part of his conquests were relinquished. It is true that Bolesław Schiefmund (Bolesław the Wry-Mouthed), who lived from 1102 to 1138, succeeded in temporarily delaying the decay of the Polish kingdom. But after his death the realm was distributed among his four sons, and a decline began that was to continue for two centuries. The Silesian and the West Pomeranian princes paid feudal duty to the German emperor.

A Polish Duke Calls for German Assistance

The most important single historical event of that period was the intervention of the German Order (Teutonic Order of Knights) in the battles between the Poles and the — at that time still un-

Christianized — Pruzzen. Duke Conrad of Masovia in the year 1225 called on the German Order for assistance, as alone he could not defend himself against the Pruzzen; and in return he presented the Culmerland to the Order. In 1226, the Holy Roman Emperor Frederick II certified the Order's possession of this area "along with all further conquests", in the Golden Bull of Rimini. This sanctioning by the international law of the day was followed by ecclesiastical sanctioning. In the Bull of Rieti, Pope Gregory IX certified the cession of the Culmerland to the Order by Conrad of Masovia. The Pope also designated as being under control of the Order all regions inhabited by those Pruzzen who could be won over to Christianity; as "property of St. Peter", those areas were bestowed upon the German Order for "perpetual free possession".

The feudal authority over Pomerania had already passed to Brandenburg. The Knights turned to the east, and by 1283 had united the whole area of the Pruzzen with the state administered by the Order. The *Kulmer Handfeste* issued by the Order in 1233 remained for centuries the "Magna Charta" of all German settlements in the region; thereafter they were subject to German law.

It is in this period that Memel (1252) and Königsberg (1255) were founded.

An alliance between the German Order and the Livonian Brothers of the Sword extended the jurisdiction of the German Order, from 1237 onward, to the Narowa and to the Peipu Lake.

The Revival of Poland

In this period Poland suffered severely from the invasions of the Mongols. Although a further advance westward of the Mongols was checked in the battle of Liegnitz (1241), the whole region nevertheless was laid waste. It was only under Duke Przemyslaw II, who was crowned king in Gnesen in 1295, that Poland began a new historical ascent.

After battles with the Order over Pomerelia, Casimir the Great in the Peace of Kalisch in 1343 had to recognize the Order's right of

31

ownership of the region; and finally, in the Treaties of Trentschin of 1335 and Visegrad (Hungary) of 1339, also renounced Silesia in favor of Bohemia. Nevertheless, like Bolesław Chrobry before him, he pushed far into what was known as Red Russia or the Ukraine. He conquered the provinces of Bielsk and Cholm, Galicia and Lemberg, the western Volhynia and Podolia.

> *Since the time of Casimir the Great, the German-Polish border in the Silesian area has remained unchanged through the centuries, up until the Treaty of Versailles. One and a half centuries before America was discovered this border came into existence. It has endured some 600 years — a proof of its roots in history. In the whole of Europe there is — except for the border between Spain and Portugal — no other border that has been so stable or of such long duration.*

Slavic Princes Call for German Settlers

It was not through conquest but through peaceful settlement that the country between Oder and Memel received its German stamp. German settlers, called by Slavic princes, cultivated the land, founded towns and cities according to German law, and were a major factor in the development of trade and of a general economic upsurge.

Most significant of all for the cultivation and economic development of the area was the decision taken by several Slavic princes more or less simultaneously to bring in German settlers. The beginnings of this peaceful and productive settlement go back to the middle of the 12th century. In particular the princes of Pomerelia recognized the advantages that German settlement could bring with it. Other Slavic princes followed the example. In Silesia, it was Duke Heinrich of Breslau who did most to foster immigration from Central Germany, Franconia, and Thuringia. In this way a large number of German towns and villages came into existence between the Sudeten area and the region around the mouth of the Vistula. In lower Silesia alone, some 1,500 villages and 63 cities were founded in the 13th century, and in upper Silesia well over 200 villages and about the same number of larger communities. German monks founded monasteries. To name only one among them, the Oliva monastery, known in connection with the Peace of Oliva, came into existence in 1178.

In the Prussian areas, 93 German towns were founded by the end of the 14th century. Half a century earlier, the number of villages had already surpassed 1,400.

German settlement in Pomerania took place over about the same period of time. The settlers came mainly from Mark Brandenburg, Lower Saxony, Westphalia and the Rhineland. Among the settlements were Stralsund (1234), Stettin (1243), Stargard (1235), Kolberg (1235) and Köslin (1266). It is interesting to note in the earliest recorded history of Pomerania, which was written by instruction of Duke Bogislaw X around the year 1500, an evidence that the Slavic Pomeranians by no means considered themselves to be Polish, but rather insisted on the contrary. The history contains the phrase

> ". . . ne quis nos addat Polonis"

freely translated,

> "Let nobody think to count us among the Poles!"

The Hanseatic League on the Baltic

As the area south of the Baltic Sea was being protected against invasions from the East largely by the efforts of the German Order, meanwhile east-west travel and commerce in the same area was being fostered and encouraged by the Hanseatic League.

A particularly striking example of this service to east-west trade is provided by the old German Hanse city of Danzig — which attained tragic fame after World War I as a "free city" (see Chapter 4). A steady influx of German settlers — craftsmen and merchants — helped Danzig develop in the course of the 14th century into the most important harbor along the middle reaches of the Baltic. After 1470 it played the role of a gateway to the Prussian Hanse towns. It is easier to visualize Danzig's importance at that early period if one bears in mind that the city had some 20,000 German inhabitants (aside from the numerous Slavs) at a time when so well-known a German city as Frankfurt counted only 10,000.

The German Hanseatic towns were the relay stations of the east-west trade — of a peaceful exchange of goods between the German and Slavic peoples and states, a commerce that was to mutual advantage.

> *The few dates we have just considered are evidence that the German settlement of the Eastern areas was nothing less than a genuinely European act of pioneering. This settlement, as a process of peaceful and constructive development, differs from almost any other epoch of settlement in the history of the world. Incidentally, as a further aspect of the European and international character of the German settlement, it should be noted that among its participants were not only Germans of all ethnic groups but also Englishmen, French, Dutch and Swiss.*

Poland and Lithuania Merge

A basic change occurred in the balance of political power in the East area when Grand Duke Jagiello of Lithuania was converted to Christianity (1386) and married Jadwiga, the daughter of Ludwig the Great of Poland. Poland and Lithuania thereby united their power, and formed a vise to put pressure on the area administered by the German Order. In the long run the Knights were no match for this Slavic concentration of power, which crushingly defeated the army of the Order in 1410. The decline of the Teutonic Order could now no longer be halted, particularly as the "Prussian Estates" — that is to say, the communities, cities and part of the aristocracy, bent on independence — also turned against it. In the first Peace of Thorn in 1466 the Order had to renounce its hold on Marienburg and Elbing, Pomerelia and the Ermland. It retained only one

34

part of the Prussian area. Then the administration of the Order was secularized by Albrecht of Prussia in 1525. The last Grand Masters of the Knights of the Teutonic Order finally found refuge farther to the west, in Mergentheim.

A significant development in this history is the destiny of the "Prussian Estates". After liberation from the guardianship of the Order, the estates attained autonomy, with a regional parliament (Landtag) of their own, and their own administrative law. They subjected themselves to the sovereignty of the Polish king only under certain given conditions. The king, for his part, specifically recognized their complete independence, freeing them from any obligation of military service for Poland.

Similar conditions were valid for Danzig, too. Its rights were stipulated in the "privilegium Kasimirianum" in 1457: free from taxes and customs, the right to enact its own legislation. Danzig was even granted the right to direct its own foreign policy. This *privilegium* remained the basis of Danzig's independence until its reunification with Prussia in 1793.

It is true that Polish attempts have never been lacking, in line with the policy of a "push toward the sea", to make Poland the master of the area that was later West Prussia (the "Polish Corridor" after the first world war). Within the framework of the "Lublin Union" the rights granted to the Prussian estates were rendered illusory. In order to bring Danzig into his power, King Stefan Batory even attacked the Hanse town by force of arms; his army had to withdraw, however, after a protracted siege, with no success. The people of Danzig had successfully defended their independence against their "sovereign"!

Silesia and Bohemia Under One Crown

While in the Prussian territory the characteristic of historic development was the opposition between the German Order on one hand and Poland on the other, the history of the Silesian area was marked by the rivalry between Poland and the Czechs.

35

After the turning back of the Mongol onrush in 1241 at Liegnitz, the divisions that came with inheritance gradually formed quite a number of small Silesian principalities — between 1248 and 1350 there were a dozen! The Silesians sought and obtained the backing of the King of Bohemia against the Poles. In four different treaties between 1335 and 1372 the Polish kings finally renounced all claims to Silesia. The Silesian sovereigns and dukes rendered homage to King John of Bohemia as their feudal lord, until the Habsburgs by acquiring the Bohemian crown also became the sovereigns of Silesia.

Although this development united Silesia and Bohemia under one crown, the internal differences between the two countries continued to exist; and the contrast was deepened when in the course of the Reformation Silesia became prevailingly Protestant while Bohemia remained Catholic. In 1523 there again appeared the tendency for the Silesians to detach themselves from Bohemia — although by no means in order to unite with Poland. In that year, Margrave Georg of Ansbach-Bayreuth acquired the Duchy of Jägerndorf and Friedrich II of Liegnitz-Brieg and Wohlau concluded a treaty of succession with the Margrave of Brandenburg. It was on this treaty of succession that Frederick the Great later based his action of 1740 in occupying Silesia and in opposing Maria Theresia in the two Silesian Wars. Under the Peace of Berlin, Silesia as far as the Oppa and the County of Glatz was joined to the kingdom of Prussia.

Reformation and Counter-Reformation

As in Silesia, the Reformation gained ground in Pomerania and in the Prussian area in the 16th century. In Danzig, a Christian spirit of reconciliation prevailed as the churches, including the world-famed Marienkirche, changed authority. This peaceful transformation incidentally preserved a priceless treasure of ecclesiastical garments, which remained in the Protestant Marienkirche, and survived all the turbulent eras to come up to the second world war. Only in Rome is a similarly valuable collection of garments, woven of Oriental brocades, to be found.

36

At this time too the Albertus University was founded in Königsberg; it was to become a center of intellectual life for the whole east of Germany.

In Pomerania, Pomerelia and Prussia the subsequent period of the Counter-Reformation brought with it no basic changes. These areas remained prevailingly Protestant. Silesia, however, was severely affected by the to-and- fro fighting of the Thirty Years' War. Catholicism, nourished from Bohemia, regained considerable ground there.

In West Prussia religious liberty prevailed from an early date. In general the German settlers were Protestants and the Poles Catholics.

Poland's Development to a Constitutional Monarchy

By the time Poland's so-called Jagiellon dynasty died out in 1572, this line of sovereigns had, it is true, pushed the borders of Poland far to the north and east. (Not only Prussian territory, but also the Baltic area up to the northern parts of Esthonia, had temporarily become a Polish feudal holding; and to the east and southeast the borders of Poland reached far into the White Ruthenian and Ukrainian areas). But the kingdom lacked inner cohesion. The aristocracy or "Schlachta" asserted its independence of the king, took power into its own hands, and in so doing did not always administer its holdings to best advantage. Both within and without, the reputation of the Polish state declined. The Ukrainian Cossacks, sworn enemies of the Poles, threw off Polish rule in a rebellion and sought protection from the Russians (1654). In the Nordic War, Poland lost a large part of her eastern conquests. In the Peace of Wehlau, the Great Elector of Brandenburg received sovereignty over the Duchy of Prussia and in the Peace of Oliva (1660) Poland had to cede the Baltic area to Sweden. A war with Russia ended in the Peace of Andrussow with the loss of Smolensk and Seweria as well as of the greater part of the Ukraine, uncluding Kiev.

Both Poland's complete impotence on the international scene and her worsening state of internal disorganization set the stage for the various partitions, from 1772 to 1795. Russia absorbed the lion's share of Poland. Looking back one can at least say with historical hindsight that the participation of Austria and Prussia in this reorganization of the Polish area of Europe prevented the complete swallowing of Poland by the Russian Empire of the Czar. Significant parts of Poland remained beyond the Russian borders.

At the Congress of Vienna in 1815, "Congress Poland" was united with the Czar's empire in a personal union. Earlier, in 1794, the Poles under Kościuszko had rebelled against the Russians. They rebelled again in 1831 and once more in 1863-64. The uprisings were crushed and numerous Poles had to emigrate.

Between the Thirty Years' War and World War I

> "The general rights of the human being are based on the natural freedom to be able to seek and promote his own welfare — without infringing on the rights of others. Mutual promises must be holy to the state as well as to its citizens."
> — from the General Prussian Common Law of March 20, 1794.

> "The Sovereign is the first servant of his state."
>
> Frederick the Great

The Peace of Osnabrück and Münster ended the Thirty Years' War in 1648. The whole of Germany needed a long time to recover from the severe damage of these disastrous years. Hither Pomerania to the Oder and the island of Usedom at that time belonged to Sweden. East Pomerania and Prussia were subordinated to the Elector of Brandenburg.

During the Northern War, Prussia had been invaded by Tatars; moreover, a plague had swept the country, decimating the population. The Prussian King Friedrich Wilhelm I tried to overcome the economic decay. He encouraged new settlers to come from West German lands. Swiss citizens, too, heeded his call, and in particular Salzburg religious refugees (1713). So it was that within three decades the East Prussian population increased from about 400,000 to 600,000.

In 1720, with the Peace of Stockholm, Western Pomerania joined Prussia. With the help of an influx of West German settlers, 160 new towns and villages were founded there. But this economic reconstruction suffered new setbacks, again and again, from new entanglements in war, as for example the Seven Years' War. It should be noted that as early as this war East Prussia had to submit to a Russian occupation. It is true that under a Russian governor the regional authorities still kept a relative degree of independence; but tendencies were becoming evident of an effort to incorporate the area into the empire of the Czar. Meanwhile, of course, the financial burdens on the area were quite heavy. It was only because of unexpected circumstances — the death of the Czarina Elizabeth, bringing a change in events which was the salvation of Frederick the Great — that the Russians withdrew from East Prussia. Thenceforth, the economic reconstruction program of the "Retablissements" was carried on, with Prussian thoroughness and with a good measure of success.

The Poles Under Prussian Rule in Silesia

When Silesia had finally gone into Prussian possession in the Peace of Hubertusburg, clarification was needed of how the new Prussian citizens of Polish nationality were to be treated. Bilingual teachers solved the language problem satisfactorily. And the mutual association and residence of Germans and Poles soon led to a far-reaching assimilation. It was the taking over of German expressions into Polish everyday speech that created the so-called *Wasserpolnisch* — "water Polish". Educated Poles also adopted German as their language of everyday use. The religious denominations enjoyed completely equal rights. A system of agricultural credits helped remove the indebtedness that burdened landed and agricultural properties. State credits promoted home-building. The favorable effect of all these measures showed itself in a general rise in the standard of living. It is small wonder that the Poles felt comfortable under Prussian administration. The Polish rebellions against the Russians, mentioned above, failed to find a single answering echo in Upper Silesia, in the population of which Poles were strongly intermingled.

The same is true for the Masurians and Kaschubians in West Prussia. They too saw no reason to end their adherence to the Prussian state. They did not identify themselves with the nationalist slogans of the Polish rebels against Czarist Russian rule. Even at the time of the so-called *Kulturkampf*, the struggle between the state and the Roman Catholic church, in Bismarck's day, the Polish residents' lack of motivation to break away was evident. The tension between church and state originated in West and South Germany and spread to East Germany. In the areas where Poles had their homes, however, the conflict remained a socio-cultural struggle; it did not become a political or national issue.

Danzig a Free City for the First Time

At the time of Poland's first division, Prussia had attempted to incorporate Danzig, but had not been able to carry this plan against the Russians. Only at the time of the second partition did Prussia attain her goal: Danzig, together with Thorn and the area between, joined Prussia as "West Prussia".

It was during the Napoleonic Wars that Danzig's status as a "free city" was recognized for the first time. At that time, France, represented by General Rapp, exercised the supreme authority over the free city. The collapse of the Napoleonic power ended this short episode. At the Vienna Congress of 1815, the borders of the Prussian east provinces were fixed anew through decision of the European Powers; West Prussia, with Danzig, was again united with Prussia.

This decision at Vienna, not the partitions of 1772 and 1793, is the basis in international law for West Prussia's and Posnania's belonging to Prussia. It was not an annexation, disputed by international law, but a peace treaty solemnly concluded by the European Powers, that guaranteed Germany's eastern borders until the Treaty of Versailles.

During this whole era the German East experienced an upsurge, economically, culturally and socially, with the progress of Prussia as a nucleus for the upward development. Meanwhile, however, Poland had fallen on difficult days, ever since the decline of the *Jagiellones* dynasty. A historian characterizes the contrast as follows:

> "As Europe moved forward with ever quicker footsteps, as political relationships became ever more distinct, as philosophic thought developed and the natural sciences flourished, meanwhile Poland sank into the abyss of an intellectual and political twilight".

Alexander Brückner

The First World War

The first world war confronted Poles with exceptionally confusing situations and difficult choices. Polish soldiers fought on both sides. They were to be found in the ranks of the fighting forces of the Russians, the Germans, the Austrians, the French, the British, and finally also the Americans. For whose victory should the Polish people strive and hope? A Russian defeat seemed to offer the earliest prospect for restoration of an independent Polish state. For that reason the Poles in general welcomed the German and Austrian advances, with the creation, for purposes of military administration, of the "Government-General Warsaw" and of the adjacent "Upper East Region" *(Land Ober-Ost).*

But at the same time influential spokesmen for Polish emigrés, particularly in America, began making territorial demands for

Poland that included German areas — regions in which there was no doubt that the Poles were only a minority of the population. Thus, in 1916, for example, an atlas was published by E. v. Romer in which East Prussia, West Prussia, Posnania and more than half of Silesia were claimed for the newly-to-be-founded Poland of the future.

Roman Dmwoski, a prominent Polish politician of that day, extended these demands still further by including large parts of Pomerania. Under his plan, Lithuania was to receive the eastern part of Prussia. From the area around Königsberg an independent republic was to be formed, linked with Poland by a customs union. And Danzig was to be turned over to Poland to provide "access to the sea".

In German quarters, suggestions of this kind were not taken seriously, because they seemed on their face to be so distanced from reality. Nevertheless, German and Austrian politicians of the time pondered the question of fostering the establishment of an independent Polish state with close ties to the Central Powers. Father to this thought was the wish to be able to augment the military potential of the Central Powers by recruiting Polish soldiers.

From the Austrian side, efforts were made to unite the conquered Polish territory with Galicia. However, the final decision was for the establishment of an independent Kingdom of Poland.

But the German-Austrian proclamation of this kingdom on November 5, 1916, found no response among the Polish population. Nor did hopes of an influx of Polish military recruits materialize for the Central Powers. Equally unsuccessful were efforts to establish a tripartite regency council. After the Bolshevist revolution of 1917, in fact, the Polish Socialists, with their secret "Polish military organization", became outright opponents of the Central Powers. The end of the first world war put an end to all German-Austrian plans to win an ally in an independent Poland.

Instead, President Wilson took up the plan. In 1918 the American President proclaimed his famous Fourteen Points. Point No. 13 called for the establishment of an independent Polish state *"which should include the territories inhabited by indisputably Polish populations, which should be assured a free and secure access to the sea."*

Chapter 4:

POLAND AND GERMANY IN OUR TIME

On November 11, 1918, Piłsudski proclaimed the Polish Republic in Warsaw. A few months later, on June 28, 1919, the Treaty of Versailles disposed of substantial areas of the German Eastern Territories.

What Poland Won Without Plebiscites

The following areas were removed from German jurisdiction without a plebiscite:

1. The Memel area. Until 1923 it was under Allied control. Then — with the qualification that it retained local autonomy — it was turned over to the Lithuanians in 1924.

2. Soldau and its environs. This area was awarded to Poland.

3. Danzig and surrounding territory. Danzig was made a "free city" against the expressed will of the Danzig population. The "free city" status was assigned to the area after the Poles had asked to absorb Danzig. Their demand was rejected, and the British Prime Minister, Lloyd George, referred to the clearly German character of the city.

4. The larger part of the province of Posnania. It was awarded to Poland.

5. The larger part of the province of West Prussia. It was used to form the "Polish Corridor". This corridor separated the German Reich from East Prussia without consideration of the wishes of the population concerned. The goal was the victors' wish to grant Poland an unimpeded access to the sea*.

6. The eastern part of the province of Posnania. It underwent the same fate as West Prussia.

7. Parts of four districts of Lower Silesia. These, too, were awarded to Poland.

These territorial changes withheld from more than four million people the right of self-determination. No plebiscite was held, since the victorious Powers were well aware that the population of these areas would never have voluntarily joined the newly established Polish state. Yet self-determination had been solemnly proclaimed as one of the principles of postwar settlement.

Plebiscites were held only where the presence of a considerable Polish population left open the possibility of granting Poland's territorial desires in a legal way, through exercise of self-determination.

Plebiscites were held:

1. In East Prussia for the entire governmental district of Allenstein and for parts of the district of Gumbinnen.

2. In West Prussia for the districts of Marienburg, Marienwerder, Rosenberg and Stuhm, where some Cashubians were among the population.

---

* Various solutions, including an internationally guarnteed passage, were considered. Polish spokesmen insisted, however, that a corridor under Polish sovereignty was the one arrangement that could be defended in event of war.

3. In Upper Silesia for the greater part of the industrial area that had still been left with the German Reich.

In all these territories there were populations that had had opportunity in elections for the Reichstag to vote in complete secrecy for any of the competing parties. The percentage of votes garnered by the Polish party had always been small in comparison with the support given to the German parties campaigning in the same areas. Poland's politicians knew this very well; and accordingly they took steps in advance of the plebiscites to try to influence the population and prevent the otherwise-to-be-expected unfavorable outcome for Poland.

The Polish "Activists" in Upper Silesia

On August 17, 1919, Korfanty, a former member of the German Reichstag, launched the first Polish uprising with the goal of incorporating the whole of Upper Silesia into Poland. The outbreak occurred even though the prevailingly French occupation troops had instructions from the League of Nations to maintain order in the Upper Silesian electoral area. The French were far from hostile to the Polish rebels — nevertheless, the uprisings failed to come off as planned.

On January 10, 1920, the Versailles Treaty took effect, and from this date onward all its territorial and other provisions were valid in international law.

On July 11, 1920, the plebiscites were held in the East and West Prussian areas mentioned above.

In the East Prussian electoral area, 97.8 % of those entitled to vote voted for Germany, and only 2.1 % for Poland (363,209 German, 7,980 Polish votes).

In the West Prussian area, 92.28 % voted for Germany and only 7.57 % for Poland (96,894 German, 7,947 Polish votes).

The Conference of Ambassadors accordingly decided on August 12, 1920, that the regions in question might remain with Germany.

What Poland Won Despite Plebiscites

Now it seemed clear that an uninfluenced vote in Upper Silesia would probably have the same crushing results for Poland as it had had in East and West Prussia. So Polish insurgents under Korfanty staged a second rebellion, which began on August 17, 1920, with the object of taking over control of Upper Silesia. In fact, in view of the "benevolent reserve" of the French occupation troops, they succeeded in bringing into their power a part of the industrial region of Upper Silesia. The English and Italian occupation troops meanwhile endeavored to maintain a "correct" attitude.

The plebiscite could not be held before March 20, 1921. In spite of the terror practiced by the Korfanty-organized gangs, under the eyes of the Allied Control Commission, this is the way the voting went in Upper Silesia:

For Germany — about 60 %
For Poland   — about 40 %

(719,348 votes for Germany, 479,474 votes for Poland.)

Under the circumstances, the appropriate step would have been to leave Upper Silesia with Germany, according to the will of the majority, while assuring broad cultural guarantees and rights for the Polish minority. Such a decision was feared by Korfanty and his ideological comrades. In order to create a fait accompli before the Conference of Ambassadors could act according to the election result, the third Polish rebellion was staged, on May 3, 1921. Only the employment of the German Free Corps was able to fend off the Polish attack. On May 21, 1921, the main strategic point of the Polish "front", the Annaberg, was taken by the German Free Corps, and this action checked a further advance by the insurgents.

After hesitating for some time, the Conference of Ambassadors decided on October 20, 1921, that Upper Silesia should be divided. Poland received the most important part of the industrial region — an area that comprised 47 % of the electoral district and almost a million inhabitants, the majority of whom did not want to be separated from Germany. A 15-year-long German-Polish transitional arrangement was concluded over partitioned Upper Silesia, the so-called "Geneva Convention".

The Disposition of Pomerania

In 1938 the area of the border province Posnania/West Prussia that lay north of the Netze was united with Pomerania. This area was combined with the districts of Friedberg and Arnswalde as well as with the Pomeranian districts of Dramburg and Neustettin in the governmental district of Schneidemühl.

Since 1945, eastern Pomerania has been "under Polish administration". Western Pomerania was merged administratively with Mecklenburg, part of the Soviet Zone of occupation, in order, as the plan went, to get rid of the name and concept of "Pomerania" once and for all.

The Struggle for Danzig's Independence

Not in agreement with the Versailles settlement of the matter of "Polish access to the sea", Poland systematically tried to extend her rights in the Free City of Danzig — by a "generous interpretation" of regulations and by an evasion of inconvenient provisions. The "Paris Treaty" concluded between Poland and the Free City of Danzig on November 9, 1920, formed the foundation for the Free City's relations with Poland. But in practice those relations were more like a constant state of tension. Against their will, the inhabitants of Danzig had to cede certain vital sovereign rights to Poland; in exchange, the League of Nations underwrote the independence of the free city and the protection of its constitution. Continual Polish attempts to extend to the disadvantage of Danzig those Polish rights that were not outlined clearly enough in the Paris Treaty led to permanent conflict, which created a great deal of trouble for the various High Commissioners of the League of Nations in their role as arbitrators. In the period we are reviewing, the Danzig question was never absent from the agenda of the League of Nations Council.

Poland Pushes Her Border Far to the East

Unfulfilled wishes of the Poles in the West and the North turned the ambitions of Polish statesmen toward the East. The Bolshevist revolution opened up various potentialities, and Poland tried to profit from them. In a war against Soviet Russia, the Poles after initial setbacks, were victorious, largely thanks to support from France. For in February 1921 a Polish-French defensive alliance had been concluded, and now it redounded to Poland's advantage. In the Peace of Riga of March 17, 1921, the Polish east border was pushed forward far beyond Grodno, Pinsk and Lemberg into the White Russian and Ukrainian regions.

> *The population of the regions annexed by Poland was not consulted. Nor was the population consulted when Poland in a lightning stroke took possession of Vilna and the surrounding area belonging to Lithuania. Neither the Conference of Ambassadors nor the League of Nations prevented this unilateral action by Poland. On the contrary, the Conference of Ambassadors, two years later, on March 15, 1923, recognized the new eastern border of Poland that had been fixed in the Peace of Riga.*

It is worth noting, incidentally, that some years later Poland pursued the same kind of tactics when she participated in the partition of Czechoslovakia, and in October 1938 occupied the Olsa region.

In order to become independent of Danzig as her one point of access to the sea, and at the same time to be able to exert economic pressure on the Free City of Danzig, Poland began in 1924 to build up Gdynia — until then an insignificant fishers' village in the Bay of Danzig — into a great Baltic Sea port. At Gdynia the Polish navy was to have its stronghold. Interestingly, however, Poland did not use Gdynia for her transport of ammunition and explosives, on grounds that such cargo was too dangerous to be handled there. Instead she had recourse to her treaty right to transship goods of all categories at Danzig, and unloaded this military freight in the Free City. None of Danzig's appeals to the League of Nations to alter this situation was successful. Poland reserved for herself an ammunition-unloading depot at the entrance to Danzig harbor on the Westerplatte — an area that actually served as a camouflaged naval base. It was at Westerplatte that the conflicts began which led to the second world war.

That war might come about in somewhat this way was foreshadowed by utterances of the French Marshal Foch — along with many others who saw that the Versailles settlement regarding Polish-German relations contained the nucleus of serious conflicts. After Versailles, Marshal Foch had pointed his finger at the "Polish Corridor" on a map of eastern Europe and said:

"Here lie the causes of the next war!"

Developments Up to the Second World War

Men of intellectual honesty and political good will in many nations saw the inherent dangers in the Treaty of Versailles, and the treaty's shortcomings have been discussed by many a historian. Democratic statesmen such as Germany's Stresemann and France's Briand tried hard during the 1920s to improve the European situation, not so much for the sake of Germany as in the interests of fair play and world peace. But before much could be accomplished,

49

Hitler had seized power in Germany. Beyond doubt, his demagogic appeal to many shortsighted persons was based largely on his promise of action to undo the wrongs of Versailles, wrongs that many non-German historians have recorded. Unlike the democratic statesmen who had been working on the same problem, Hitler, as the world now knows to its sorrow, "corrected" the situation by the imposition of new injustices.

As soon as he had taken domestic measures to silence his democratic opposition, Hitler began making foreign-policy moves. He got rid of the political and military restrictions that Versailles had imposed on the German Reich. As he was doing so, he had his eye on the Soviet Union as the principal and ultimate opponent. Expecting eventually to come into conflict with the U. S. S. R., he wanted to prepare the ground. He took several moves to serve this purpose.

First, on January 26, 1934, he concluded a ten-year non-aggression pact with Poland — so as to remove any interference with his plans to do away with "discrimination" against Germany in the West. Later, when he judged that the time had come to prepare his campaign against the Soviet Union, he took steps to clear the way for his effort in the East. He "solved" his Czechoslovakian problem; the events that led to the Munich Conference and subsequently to the abolition of Czechoslovakia as an independent state need not be retold here. Then, on October 24 and November 19, 1938, he transmitted to the Polish Ambassador in Berlin his proposals for a new situation in Danzig and the Polish Corridor. Danzig was to return to Germany, and extraterritorial railways and highways were to provide a direct link between the rest of the German Reich and East Prussia, across the Polish Corridor. Such a settlement — leaving aside for a moment the matter of Hitler and his international methods — would have corresponded to the repeatedly expressed will of the people of Danzig, who beyond doubt wanted to be part of Germany once more. But the problem of the Corridor would hardly have been settled.

In any case, Poland showed no readiness to agree to the proposals. Lithuania, on the other hand, on March 22, 1939, declared her readiness to return the Memel area. Again, Hitler's almost unbelievable record of violence and unilateral action has tended to obscure the rights and wrongs of the situations that he — in his unilateral and utterly reprehensible way — sought to "correct". The people of Memel, for example, like those of Danzig, had consistently indicated — since long before the arrival of Hitler on the scene — that they considered their detachment from the German homeland as an injustice that had been forced upon them. On April 3, 1939, Memel was once more incorporated into East Prussia, with retention by Lithuania of a free port in the area.

Meanwhile, the Polish government was undecided whether to accept or reject Hitler's proposals. Poland decided first to try to obtain a British guarantee of Poland's then-existing borders. The Polish effort was crowned with success: On March 31, 1939, London gave Warsaw the requested guarantee, and on April 6, 1939, the British-Polish mutual-assistance pact was concluded. Now that Poland had the backing she had sought, Foreign Minister Beck made public the contents of the German proposals, on April 23. The British Government, in other words, had concluded a pact with Poland without having been informed of the content of Hitler's proposals.

Immediately afterward, when Poland rejected the Hitler plan. Hitler gave notice of cancellation of the German-Polish non-aggression pact, on April 28, 1939. The course Hitler would choose was now becoming clearer. As had Great Britain, France ranged herself on the side of Poland, and, on July 1, 1939, rejected any change of the status quo in Danzig or the Corridor.

At the same time, the Western Powers tried to obtain the support of the Soviet Union in the event of an armed contest with the National Socialist dictatorship in Germany. To gain this support, they were ready to make sweeping concessions to the U. S. S. R. In fact, on July 24, 1939, the Western negotiators in Moscow initiated an agreement that would have opened up possibilities for Soviet influence in the Baltic states. But the agreement never took effect. For Moscow played a double game: It arrang-

51

ed for its own future advantage by agreeing to proposals that Hitler conveyed to Stalin via Ribbentrop.

So it was that on August 23, 1939, the people of the world — and not least the people of Germany — were astonished to learn that a pact stipulating non-aggression and mutual consultation had been concluded between the Third Reich and the Soviet Union. This pact practically put the Baltic states at the disposition of the Soviet Union, and in return Hitler received from Stalin a free hand in Poland. Hitler was persuaded that his pact with Moscow would dissuade the Western Powers from implementing their pledges made to Poland. He thought he could risk a "small war" against Poland, with the outcome of a foregone conclusion in view of the superiority of the German armed forces.

Hitler had, of course, thoroughly deceived himself. In the wake of his order to attack Poland on September 1, 1939, a terrible disaster unfolded, taking as its victims not only the Polish and the German people, but most peoples of the civilized world. By trying to rearrange the map of central Europe for his own convenience, Hitler managed only to prove once more that in international relations two wrongs do not make a right.

Chapter 5:

HOW THE ODER-NEISSE LINE
CAME TO BE

The place was Yalta and the time was February 1945. The conferees were President Roosevelt, Prime Ministers Churchill and Stalin, and their advisers. Discussing the provisional eastern frontiers of Poland, Soviet Foreign Minister Molotov suggested agreement on "the return to Poland of her ancient frontiers in East Prussia and on the Oder."

President Roosevelt asked how long it had been since these lands were Polish.

Mr. Molotov replied: very long ago, but they had once been Polish.

Said the U.S. President, laughing, to the British Prime Minister: "Perhaps you would want us back?"

Replied the British Prime Minister: "Well, you might be as indigestible for us as it might be for the Poles if they took too much German territory."

*Prime Minister Stalin withdrew the Soviet proposal.**

In that war year of 1945, however, events were on the side of Stalin's plans for central Europe. Backed by the Red Army, he put

---

* Yalta Documents (U.S.), p. 905. Ibid., Matthews notes, p. 911. Cited in Herbert Feis, "Churchill, Roosevelt, Stalin" (Princeton and London, 1957), p. 520.

into effect a scheme to bring about Poland's westward expansion into lands that had been German for centuries. Unfortunately, Stalin found Poles who were ready, after a time, to cooperate with him.

While history will forever recall the whole dark chapter of Hitler's aggression against Poland as a tragedy, it is also a historical fact that the Polish Government tried to make of the tragedy in Europe an occasion for the postwar aggrandizement of Poland.

After the occupation of Poland by German troops, the Polish government in Warsaw withdrew to London. There and elsewhere the Polish exiles lost no opportunity to press on the Allies their demands for a greater Poland, to be carved from German territory.

As we shall see, the Polish claims played into the hands of Moscow. For the Soviet strategists were planning two postwar goals in Europe:

(1) Westward territorial expansion by the U. S. S. R., largely at the expense of Poland — with a "compensation" to Poland at Germany's expense; and

(2) A general Communist push to the West — by domination of Poland and those other European nations that after the war were to become known as the East Bloc.

The Allied War Aims

Yet the territorial aggrandizement and the enforced changes in the governments of central and eastern Europe violated the stated war aims of the allies. On August 14, 1941, Great Britain and the United States proclaimed the Atlantic Charter:

> "First, their countries seek no aggrandizement, territorial or other; second, they desire to see no territorial changes that do not accord with the freely expressed wishes of the peoples concerned."

54

Later that year, both Poland and the Soviet Union signed the Charter. Along with representatives of 24 other nations, Polish and Soviet representatives reaffirmed its principles by signing the United Nations Declaration (which embodied the Atlantic Charter) in Washington on January 1, 1942.

Thus the changes that have been forced upon eastern and central Europe — including the Polish occupation of German territory — are in violation of wartime pledges made by, among others, the Soviet Union and the Polish government.

Polish Territorial Ambitions

We have seen (Chapter 3) how Polish demands after the first world war drew warnings from Allied statesmen of trouble ahead. Hitler's September 1939 attack on Poland was hardly two months old when the Prime Minister of the Polish exile government, General Władysław Sikorski, began asking British and French representatives to guarantee Poland more territory after the war that was then beginning — "first of all, a longer seacoast" — than she had received in the Versailles Treaty.

A Polish government declaration to the Poles at home was made from Paris on December 20 of the same year. It spoke of a greater Poland after the war, with assurances of "free national and cultural development" to national minorities in that expanded Poland of the future.

The Polish press abroad was even freer with its plans for Poland. Thus the newspaper "Narodowiec", published in Paris, declared in its December 22 issue that "After the present war with Germany, Poland must keep, among other things, East Prussia, in order to be able to play the role of a haven of freedom between the Baltic and the Black Sea."

The claims made by the exile Polish press included wide areas that were German, Lithuanian, Ruthenian and Ukrainian.

Lille was another center of Poles living abroad, and the "Polska Walcząca" published in that French city wrote in its edition of May 12, 1940: "The boundaries of Polish living space are: in the north the Baltic, in the west the Oder river, in the southwest the Sudetenland, in the south the Moravian Gap and the Carpathian mountains, in the southeast the Dnieper and finally in the northeast the Dvina."

Similar claims were also made by Poles living in the New World. For example, a Chicago Polish newspaper, the "Dziennik Związkowy", had this to say on December 3, 1940: "The western border of Poland must be a line that runs at least 10 kilometers west of the lower Oder and then to the Erzgebirge."

Western Insistence on a Free Poland

It is important to bear in mind, when considering the Oder-Neisse problem, a central fact that runs like a thread through the whole fabric of the Allied wartime and postwar conferences:

To the extent that the Western Allies gave a sympathetic ear to any Polish claims against Germany, they did so on the understanding that there would be a free, democratic Polish government after the war. That is what the vast majority of the long-suffering Polish people themselves wanted; that was what the Soviet Union pledged at its meetings with the Western Allies.

By free and democratic, it became clear as early as 1939, the Western Allies had in mind a regime less authoritarian than the government that Poland had known under Marshal Piłsudski. It was a breach of faith with the Western Allies for the Communists to force on postwar Poland an authoritarianism still more oppressive than that it had known in the past. Poles who are free to speak readily concede the truth of this matter.

The tentative Western Allied willingness, during the war, to favor territorial concessions to postwar Poland in a peace treaty is always to be considered along with the other half of the Western Allied

The Marienburg, an Outpost of Christianity When Europe Was Young

The huge Gothic edifice was built by the German Order (Teutonic Order of Knights) between 1275 and 1382. The Marienburg was the chief seat of the Teutonic Order from 1309 to 1457; later it and the town of Marienburg became part of West Prussia. Today it is under Polish administration. It was the Teutonic Knights who were in the vanguard of Christianity in medieval Europe. In 1225 Duke Konrad of Masovia called on the German Order for assistance, as the Poles alone found they could not hold out in battle against the — at that time still un-Christianized — tribe called the Pruzzen. In return he presented the Culmerland to the German Order. Over many decades it played a major role in the civilizing of this part of Europe. As early as 1226 the Holy Roman Emperor Frederick II certified the Order's possession of the area; so did later Pope Gregory IX. Today the Polish regime seeks to represent Polish administration of the area that includes the Marienburg as "a Polish victory over the Germans".

Built by a Medieval Master — Destroyed in Modern War

This part of the Marienburg is known as the „Plauen Bulwark" after the master-builder Heinrich von Plauen, who planned it for the defense of the Marienburg from hostile tribes. In 1945 Soviet artillery fire severely damaged this and other parts of the age-old German center in this part of Europe. The Poles who today administer the area have in part restored the historic site.

understanding with the Soviet Union: that postwar Poland would be a bulwark of democracy founded on free elections.

Much of the Western strategy at inter-allied conference tables throughout the war — and right up to the Potsdam Agreement of 1945 — was dedicated to keeping Poland a free community in the community of free nations. Since the war was being fought to overthrow a dictatorship in Germany, it would have made no sense from the Western Allied standpoint to bring about a new authoritarianism in central Europe. *Western support of Polish territorial claims was conditional on the preservation of Poland as a free and independent nation.* *

For that matter, Polish politicians' own ideas about postwar relations with Germany, including territorial arrangements, began by being more modest than they later became under the pressure of "suggestions" that originated in Moscow.

As Sikorski Saw the Future

In December 1942, Polish Prime Minister Sikorski visited President Roosevelt. During his stay in Washington, he handed Sumner Welles, the U. S. Undersecretary of State, two memoranda outlining Polish ideas about postwar settlements. **

---

* See, for example, U. S. Department of State, "Foreign Relations of the United States. Diplomatic Papers. The Conferences of Malta and Yalta 1945". Both President Roosevelt and Prime Minister Churchill energetically opposed the Oder-Neisse frontier. Page 53 records Sir Winston's famous remark: "It would be a pity to stuff the Polish goose so full of German food that it got indigestion." Even the possibility of a less extreme territorial concession was made dependent on formation of a free and independent Poland.

** The memoranda were later preserved in the General Sikorski Historical Institute in London. Excerpts were published in the London *Observer* of April 1, 1947, and in an article by Aleksander Bregman in *Dziennik Polski* of Dec. 9, 1952.

These memoranda are important not only for what they requested, but equally for what they did not request.

In the first memorandum Sikorski spoke of creating "political, economic and other conditions which would facilitate the implementation of a constructive plan for the federation of the central European countries." He suggested assignment of a northeastern part of East Prussia to Lithuania. (As events have turned out, Lithuania for all practical purposes has since been absorbed by the U.S.S.R.) The main part of East Prussia, including Königsberg, he argued, should go to Poland. (Since 1945 Königsberg and its environs have been under the provisional administration of the U.S.S.R.) He argued for the changing of the status of the Upper Silesian coal-rich area: by assigning it to Poland, by sharing it between Czechoslovakia and Poland, or by establishing an international control.

In the second of Sikorski's two memoranda to the Americans, the Polish leader made proposals for Polish *military occupation* of the German territories east of the Oder and the western Neisse rivers. He made clear, as we shall see below, that he was suggesting a limited measure — an occupation — and not the attempt at annexation that has taken place since 1945.

Two points about Sikorski's proposals are important to note:

1. He foresaw a central European federation and the possibility of international cooperation in specified areas.

A European federation implies (as it actually has come to mean, since the war, in western Europe) the minimizing at least to some degree of the importance of national boundaries. It implies international agreement on freedom of movement, of residence and of trade. This concept is reality in western Europe, with the free part of Germany a participant in the arrangement. But Sikorski's concept of 1942 is far from actuality in central Europe. The Iron Curtain, maintained since 1945 by Communist policy, not only separates free Germans from unfree Germans; it also prevents the people of Poland and other countries under Communist Bloc domination from being good neighbors either with Germany or with the rest of Europe.

58

2. *He proposed a military occupation of German areas*

In regard to postwar treatment of the Oder-Neisse region as a whole, Sikorski's second memorandum discusses a military occupation (as distinct from an annexation). In fact, the memorandum actually *draws the analogy of French occupation of the German Rhineland after the first World War.* Such a temporary, military occupation of German territory is, of course, quite another concept from what actually has taken place: In violation of the Potsdam Agreement of 1945, the Communist regime in Poland has tried to absorb outright the German areas that Poland was to administer pending a peace treaty.

Soviet Tactics Regarding Poland

Seven months after making his proposals in Washington, General Sikorski was killed when his plane crashed. He was succeeded as Polish Prime Minister by Stanisław Mikołajczyk.

Meanwhile the exaggerated claims against German territory that were appearing in the Polish exile press — we have seen samples above — served well the purposes of Moscow. For before long the Soviet Government was seen to have its own reasons for wanting the Poles to expand in the west at the expense of the Germans. In fact, strategists in Moscow, dedicated to the cause of Communist expansion, had early developed plans for Poland, for Germany, and, to the extent that it might be possible to realize them, for Europe.

It was after Hitler concluded his 1939 pact with Stalin that the German dictator felt emboldened to invade Poland. Soon the Red Army was in Poland, too. Under cover of the Stalin-Hitler accord, Moscow sent troops to occupy the areas of eastern Poland that the Soviet Union had ceded to Poland in the Peace of Riga of 1921. (See Chapter 3.)

As was soon to become evident, the Soviet Union had no intention of giving up, for a second time, those territories that Poland had acquired in 1921 and that the Red Army took back in 1939. However, when Hitler made war on Stalin in 1941, the Soviet

Union and Poland found themselves military in the same camp; so Moscow went through the motions of concluding what was called a "Normalization of Soviet-Polish Relations". On July 30, 1941, the Soviet and the Polish governments signed an accord: The Soviet Union stated that the Stalin-Hitler pact had "lost its validity" as far as the "territorial changes in Poland" were concerned.

Moscow, to be sure, wanted the Polish eastern territories — and the Red Army had not "lost its validity". But how was the Soviet Union to assert openly its claim to eastern Poland? After all, the Soviet and the Polish people were on the same side in the war. Moreover, a cornerstone of Stalin's planning for postwar Europe was the creation of a pro-Russian, that is, Communist, regime in Poland. He could hardly pose as the ally and champion of the Polish people while he was subtracting territories from Poland — not unless he made up for it to the Poles in some other way.

The "Compensation" Theory

Moscow's "some other way" was the proposal to "compensate" Poland in the west for territories that the Soviet Union was taking away from her in the east.

That "compensation" was to be the Oder-Neisse settlement that awarded Poland administration of Germany's Eastern Territories. Moscow paid lip service in 1945 to the insistence of the Western Allies that the award to Poland was only provisional pending a peace treaty. But since 1945, Soviet policy has been to argue that the German Eastern Territories became Polish by decision of the 1945 Potsdam Conference* and that the other nations of the world should recognize the Oder-Neisse Line.

Its Illogicality

It is not within the scope of this book to argue the historical rights and wrongs of the territorial dispute between Poland and the

* An impossibility under international law. (See Chapter 1.)

Soviet Union in the East. As noted above, the area was handed over to Poland by the Peace of Riga in 1921, and was taken back by Stalin in the wake of Hitler's invasion of Poland in 1939. Was Poland entitled (as almost all Poles argued vehemently in the early years of the second world war) to keep her eastern lands? If so, then she could not be "compensated" for her loss to the Soviet Union by being repaid with territories of a third power, Germany.

Or was the Soviet Union entitled (as Stalin argued) to the territories that had become Polish in 1921? If so, then Poland had no valid claims to "compensation" at all.

A Polish Warning Before Teheran

By the time of the Teheran Conference (November 28 to December 1, 1943) the Western Allies were hesitant to contradict Stalin, lest he refuse to renew his relations with the Polish government in London,* and end up by Communizing Poland. At this point the Americans and the British were well aware of Stalin's intention of claiming the part of Poland east of the so-called Curzon Line.

The "compensation" theory — the idea of giving Poland a piece of Germany in exchange for a piece of territory to be given up to the Soviet Union — was discussed. On December 1, at the final session, Prime Minister Churchill put on the record that "the actual tracing of the frontier line requires careful study".

While the question of Poland's westward expansion was under consideration, Stalin put forward his claim to the "warm-water port of Königsberg" — also German. He remarked that if the Russians got this area, they would "have Germany by the throat".

Ironically, the record shows that the Poles themselves saw the danger in unreasonable expansion westward at German expense. The exile government exposed Stalin's long-range intentions, in a mem-

---

* Broken off after that government requested an international investigation of the mass murder of Polish officers in Katyn Forest. Moscow rejected Sikorski's request for a visit to the scene by an International Red Cross commission.

orandum of October 8, 1943, from the Polish Ambassador in London to the U. S Secretary of State:

> "... even though the Soviet government should, in compensation (for Poland's territorial losses to Russia in the east), support Polish claims to some German territories in the West, these new frontiers would make Poland dependent on her eastern neighbor, and enable the Soviet Union to use her as a springboard for extending its domination over Central Europe and Germany in particular."

Immediately after the Teheran Conference, the Poles in London protested to the United Nations that the Soviet Union clearly did not intend to respect Poland's territorial integrity.

Soviets Urge Westward Expansion

Far from denying the truth of the Polish protest, the Soviet Government tried to square things with the Poles by propagandizing the theory of territorial compensation. In an attempt to divert Polish attention from what was happening to eastern Poland, Moscow dramatized opportunities for Polish expansion to the west. A Soviet statement reported by the Soviet news agency TASS on January 11, 1944, follows:

> "The opportunity is presenting itself for Poland to emerge once more as a strong and independent state. But the renaissance of Poland must not be based on the taking away of Ukrainian and White Russian territory, but rather on the return to Poland of territory that belonged to Poland for time without reckoning, and that was snatched from the Polish nation by Germany.* Poland's boundary must be expanded westward..."

But the Poles of London still did not agree to the Communist formula. They had strong reservations about an extreme westward

---

* Actually, the Polish-German border has been one of the most stable in Europe since the Middle Ages. (See Chapter 3.)

expansion. As for the area being demanded by the Soviet Union, they had said as early as December 2, 1942: "In the question of our eastern borders, the National Assembly holds firm to the basis of the Treaty of Riga."

Allies at Cross-Purposes

Thus the Allies, though united in their war against the German dictatorship, were disastrously at cross-purposes in their plans for a better postwar Europe. The Communists were absorbed in plans for territorial expansion. The Western Allies were absorbed in trying to keep as much of Europe as possible for the free world. And the Poles in exile tried once more to call attention to the danger of yielding to the Soviet initiative in the planning of postwar settlements. Prime Minister Mikołajczyk wrote to the President of the United States on March 25, 1944, objecting in strong terms to the plan to "compensate" Poland in the west for territory to be given up in the east. In his letter the Polish statesman warned that such a settlement could mean trouble "with the changing of the political situation of Europe in fifty years or so."

When Mikołajczyk wrote, he apparently did not know that part of the manoeuvre in central Europe was to be the creation of another source of future tension: the forcible expulsion of Germans from the German territories to be placed under Polish administration.

Long since, the Western Allies had themselves become filled with misgivings over the course that events were taking in central Europe. They began to look forward to cooler and fairer European settlements at a peace conference (which at this writing has not yet been held). Thus, the British Foreign Secretary, Anthony Eden, told the House of Commons:

> "It is better not to discuss this thing further until the war is over and the victorious powers have gathered around the peace table."

But the Communists were not waiting for the peace conference. They made moves to create a fait accompli. On July 26, 1944, the Soviet Government made an agreement with the Polish Communists, who were about to establish their "Polish Committee of National Liberation" at Lublin. The Moscow agreement with the Lublin Communists included recognition of the Curzon Line as Poland's eastern border. In return, Moscow "guaranteed" that Poland's new western frontiers would be on the Oder and western Neisse rivers. Moreover, the July 1944 agreement turned over administration of the Russian-occupied areas of Poland to the Lublin committee. Then, on August 8, 1944, the leader of the pro-Communist Socialists in Poland, Osóbka-Morawski, announced a demand for the Oder-Neisse frontier at a press conference.

Thus the summer of 1944 saw Moscow making a deal with its Communist puppets in "liberated" Poland: German territory was "offered" to the future Poland (although under international law there could be no thought of such a unilateral "offer") in return for cession to the Soviet Union of territory in Poland's east. Stalin's tactic, of course, was to reinforce the position of the Communists in Poland and to reward them in the west for their sacrifice in the east. Above all, he made use of the Lublin committee to bring Poland under the Soviet Russian sphere of influence.

13th Century German Architecture in Königsberg

The German Order (Teutonic Order of Knights) built this castle in 1255 on the bank of the river Pregel. Later several settlements in the area united to form Königsberg. The Western Allies at Potsdam in 1945 indicated they would support at a future peace conference a Soviet Russian wish to take over Königsberg. Meanwhile, however, the Russians have renamed the city Kaliningrad, without bothering to wait for the peace conference that the Potsdam conferees intended should settle Germany's borders. Königsberg, traditionally a flourishing city of Germany and Europe, before World War II counted 370,000 inhabitants. It was for centuries a member of the peacefully trading North European partnership of free cities called the Hanseatic League.

The Albertus University in Königsberg:
Immanuel Kant Taught Here

The old university at Königsberg was founded by the Germans in 1544. Immanuel Kant, famed for his doctrine of the categorical imperative — live as you would wish everybody to live — is buried here (site below).

As it turned out, Moscow's dealings — backed by the presence of the Red Army — with the Polish Communists of Lublin were to spell the doom of the Polish government in exile in London.

At first the "compensation" idea — giving Poland a slice of Germany in return for a slice of territory given up to the U. S. S. R. — had been turned down "by every responsible Pole in the West and in occupied Poland".* But eventually the idea of accepting a large piece of Germany was taken up by the Polish Communists — who themselves, it may be remembered, had no real freedom of action when instructions came from above and from Moscow.

Renewed Polish Protest

But the Poles in London were still free to protest, and they did. Prime Minister Mikołajczyk and his Cabinet in exile for a long time refused to accept the proffered deal: a Polish eastern frontier based on the so-called Curzon Line and a Polish western frontier based deep within Germany, on the Oder-Neisse Line.

Another prominent Polish politician in exile was the anti-Communist Socialist, Arciszewski. He too said no. Like the other Polish politicians of World War II (and like, before them, the Polish politicians at the time of the Versailles Treaty), he was ready to see his homeland expanded at Germany's expense. But he was not prepared for the extreme westward expansion that the Polish regime has claimed for itself since 1945. In an interview published in the Sunday Times (London) on December 17, 1944, Arciszewski said: "... we do not want to expand our frontier in the west to include 8 to 10 million Germans". He specifically disavowed claims to "either Breslau or Stettin" — both of which, as it turned out, actually did come under Polish control in 1945. Nor did he mention at the time (either because he was unaware of it or wanted nothing

* Zoltan Michael Szaz, "Germany's Eastern Frontiers", Chicago, 1960. See also Stanisław Mikołajczyk, "The Pattern of Soviet Domination", London, 1948.

to do with it) a plan for a mass expulsion of Germans from the affected areas.

But whatever the Poles in London said or did not say, demanded or did not demand, conceded or did not concede, by now mattered little. For Stalin in that same winter recognized the Communist-dominated Lublin committee as the provisional government of Poland. And as the Red Army advanced westward, Polish Communists, encouraged by Moscow, grew more demanding in their claims for "compensation" from Germany.

Indeed, with the Red Army in command in eastern Europe, it remained only for future Allied conferences — Yalta and Potsdam — to put as good a face as possible on the Communist fait accompli; and, important above all from the Western standpoint, to *place on the record of these international conferences the fact that the Polish-German situation was provisional until conclusion of a peace treaty.*

Geographical Problems at Yalta

Stalin, Churchill and Roosevelt met for the last time at Yalta in the Crimea, from February 4 to 11, 1945. Since then it has often been pointed out that the Western Allies were not in the best possible bargaining position vis-a-vis the Soviet Union: They were eager to obtain Russian help against Japan, and meanwhile most of Europe except for Bohemia, Moravia and Slovakia had come under the control of the Red Army.

Not only was the Soviet government in the driver's seat as to the principle of the Polish-German settlement; it also felt able to insist on having its way as to details — details that were to affect the lives of many millions of people and the future of Europe.

Aided by the vagueness of earlier Allied discussions, Stalin maintained at Yalta that he had all along favored the Western Neisse river as part of Poland's boundary. "In these general discussions", says Churchill in his memoirs about the Yalta Conference,

66

"maps were not used and the distinction between the Eastern and Western Neisse did not emerge as clearly as it should have done." *

Minutes taken of the discussion in the third plenary session of the Yalta Conference record Stalin as saying: "I prefer that the war continue a little longer and give Poland compensation in the west at the expense of Germany ... There are two Neisse rivers, the east and the west. I favor the west."

This offhand way of regarding the future frontiers of two peoples who had been neighbors since the dawn of European history seems alarming, in retrospect. As a matter of fact, the approach was even then causing concern among Western Allied experts. By February 10, Churchill recalls, a telegram had arrived at Yalta from the British War Cabinet "which strongly deprecated any reference to a frontier as far west as the Western Neisse ..."

But the Communists were taking things out of the Western Allies' hands, even as the Yalta Conference continued. On February 5, the Polish Communists announced that they had taken over "the administration" of the area up to the Oder and the Western Neisse rivers.

We have seen something of what was and is involved in the over-all arbitrariness of this German-Polish "settlement" that in reality has not been a settlement. Let us pause to see what was involved in even a detail of that settlement: What was the difference, for the purposes of a provisional border, between two rivers of the same name? For one thing, the large additional area bounded by the Western Neisse included several million additional Germans, and almost no Poles. These Germans, with the more than six million who lived east of the Oder, faced expulsion as a result of a few words at a conference table.

* Cchurchill, Winston S., "The Second World War", Vol. VI, p. 327.

At Yalta, let it be said clearly, both Churchill and Roosevelt refused to agree to the enlarged claim.* Not the Yalta Conference, however, but force was running things in central Europe. During the spring after Yalta, many of the Germans living in the disputed area fled before the advancing Red Army; and many of those who tried to stay were expelled, regardless of the lack of any existing international sanction for the expulsion.

Two Related Allied Pledges

It has been emphasized earlier in this chapter that the consideration given by the Western Allies to territorial concessions for Poland was always made conditional on the emergence after the war of a free Polish people. Nowhere is the tie between the two elements of this contract — territorial gains for a people who were to be a member of the democratic family of nations — to be seen more clearly than in the final decisions at Yalta. The conferees agreed that:

> 1. "The provisional government which is now functioning in Poland should . . . be reorganized on a broader democratic basis with the inclusion of democratic leaders from Poland itself and from Poles abroad." Moreover, the reorganized government *"shall be pledged to the holding of free and unfettered elections as soon as possible on the basis of universal suffrage and secret ballot."*

> 2. Poland's eastern boundary was foreseen to be the Curzon Line, with minor modifications in favor of Poland. As for Poland's western boundaries, the three Heads of Government contemplated that "Poland must receive substantial accessions of territory in the north and west". But *"the final delimitation of the western frontier of Poland"* should *"await the Peace Conference"*.

* American and British accounts alike record the Western Allies' concern over the ethnological and moral implications of the maximum Communist territorial claims against Germany. See, for example, Churchill, op cit., and Byrnes, James F., "Speaking Frankly", New York and London, 1947.

Even with these qualifications, sharp questions about the arrangement of the Polish-German situation were raised in both the British Parliament and the U. S. Congress. Churchill and Roosevelt defended the Yalta decisions as the only ones possible under the circumstances, and both pointed to the provisional character of the arrangement.

Roosevelt reassured critics that "a new government on a broader basis" was to be established in Poland, chosen by "a universal, democratic and secret vote".

"The Poles Are Going Too Far"

On February 12, the Polish regime in London was informed of the outcome at Yalta. The next day, on February 13, the Poles protested the Yalta plans as "a fifth partition of Poland, this time undertaken by her own allies".

Churchill denied the charge. Speaking in the House of Commons on February 27, 1945, he said the area east of the Curzon Line had been Russian before — and, moreover, that the Soviet Union had made great wartime sacrifices for Poland's liberation.

On the following day, Eden added that the British Government had recognized the Curzon Line as Poland's eastern border because a majority of the population in the area beyond it was not Polish.

While the Western Allies thus defended Poland's loss of territory to the Soviet Union in the east, it is to be noted that they were *not* similarly inclined to defend Poland's extreme expansion in the west. On the contrary, in his memoirs, Churchill states that he would have preferred "a public break rather than allow anything beyond the Oder and the Eastern Neisse to be ceded to Poland".*

* "Triumph and Tragedy", p. 672.

Later the same year when (on August 20) the Polish situation was being debated in the House of Commons, Anthony Eden stated:

> *"I would only say to our Polish friends that as, last time, they made a mistake in going too far East, so this time, I fear, they are making a mistake in insisting on going too far West"*.

Since World War II, the Western Allies have sometimes been accused of a "sell-out" of democracy in eastern and central Europe. But the record shows that, whatever mistakes may have been made, the West tried consistently to achieve a postwar Europe based on self-determination.

The Yalta Conference, as we have just seen, announced the principle of a democratic government for Poland. After Yalta, the Western Allies made continuing efforts to get the Soviet Union to underpin the promise with action.

Typical of these efforts was a visit by Harry Hopkins, special representative of the U. S. President, to Stalin in Moscow on May 26 and 27, 1945. At the second of their two meetings, Hopkins obtained from Stalin an affirmation that (1) the Soviet government did not intend to interfere with Polish affairs; (2) that it would not oppose the inclusion of independent political elements in the Polish government; and (3) that it would join with the American and British governments in seeing to it that the reorganized Polish government held free elections and respected individual rights and liberties.

As for the Poles in London, who at first had protested the Yalta plan for their homeland as "the fifth partition of Poland", they found themselves in a dilemma. If they continued to refuse to have anything to do with the Yalta plan, they might lose for Poland not only the lands east of the Curzon Line — an area that the Soviet Union seemed determined to keep in any case — but also the "compensatory" areas that were to be awarded to Poland (even if only provisionally, "pending a peace treaty") from Eastern

Germany. In these circumstances, the London Poles decided to go along.

On April 16, 1945, Mikołajczyk announced acceptance of the Yalta provisions — but he linked his acceptance of them, as the Allies had done, with a Poland that was to have a free, representative government.

The Poles Are Told: "Only Provisional"

The next step was to invite Polish representatives to lay the groundwork for forming such a representative Polish government. The Commission of Three (the U. S. and British Ambassadors in Moscow and Soviet Foreign Minister Molotov) issued invitations to a number of Poles to come to Moscow for discussions.

The British Ambassador, Clark Kerr, read the Yalta formulation aloud to the conferees and pointed out that the final decision on the boundary question would have to await the peace conference. On the next day, Władysław Gomulka, then chairman of the political committee of the Warsaw government, asked U. S. Ambassador Harriman what the U. S. Government thought of Polish claims in the west, in particular the inclusion of Stettin. Harriman replied that the claims would have to be talked over by the three powers (the U. S., U. K. and U. S. S. R.) and would have to be settled at the peace conference.

Regarding the new government that was formed in Poland, it was eventually, as we have seen, to be based upon free elections. These were to be held "later", when some millions of Poles had returned home from abroad. The elections have never been held. It soon developed, moreover, that the Poles returned from exile were by no means able to hold their own against the Communists in the new so-called "government of national unity". To this it should be added once more that the Polish Communists themselves were practically the prisoners of Moscow and of the Red Army.

Meanwhile, in May 1945, the Soviet authorities went still further with their strategy of trying to create a fait accompli in Central Europe. They assigned to Polish control that part of the Soviet occupation zone extending to the Oder and the Western Neisse. Vigorous protests were made by the British and American governments, but were met by evasions from Molotov.

On July 7, two days after the new Polish provisional government was recognized, General Zhukov, at the second meeting of the Allied Kommandatura for Berlin, made the Communist course still clearer. The Soviet general left no doubt that the resources east of the line formed by the Oder and the Western Neisse would not be available for Berlin or the western sections of Germany. Why? Because, he argued, Germany did not exist; and he went further: Everyone knew, said the Soviet general, that the Yalta conference had fixed the Polish frontier along that line. This, of course, was not the case, and in the period between Yalta and Potsdam the Western Allies had taken every opportunity to challenge the Soviet pretense. (As, for example, in a strongly worded memorandum prepared by George F. Kennan on request of Acting U. S. Secretary of State Joseph C. Grew and given to Andrei Vishinsky, Soviet Assistant Commissar for Foreign Affairs, on May 8.)

For their part, the British also made their stand clear on the illegality and unwisdom of the unilateral settlement of the Polish-German question. The British Foreign Office, a few days before the start of the Potsdam Conference, recorded its stand (in almost identical memoranda given by the British Embassy in Washington to the State Department on July 13 and by the Undersecretary of State for Foreign Affairs to Assistant Secretary of State Dunn on July 14 in Potsdam).

> *The British Government declared that it could scarcely be expected that British public opinion would lastingly support a settlement that amputated about one-fifth of Germany, in which about ten million Germans had formerly lived. Such action would prove to be a formidable obstacle to the maintenance of European peace.*

The American advisers at Potsdam were impressed by the British reasoning, an American historian of the proceedings chronicles.*

> *The U. S. approach was that there should be no "firm fixation of any frontier line before the peace conference met".*

As the above-quoted historian reports from official documents, the Potsdam Conference brought home to the Western Allies that "no ordinary way was left to prevent the Russians and Poles from pushing too far westward."

Stalin, of course, defended the Communist westward advance in Europe. But in doing so:

> *Stalin said once more that final decision about frontiers was to be left to the peace conference.*

The Record of Potsdam

For years the Communists have tried to pretend that the conferees at Potsdam had in mind a final, once-and-for-all settlement of the Polish-German border. As the record shows, this was simply not the case.

Failing in their pretense that all three allies at Potsdam had in mind only a provisional solution of the Oder-Neisse problem, Soviet propaganda has sometimes fallen back to the position that there was a misunderstanding at Potsdam: that although the Western Allies thought in provisional terms the Soviet Government thought in terms of a final settlement. This too, as the record shows, is not the case.

* Herbert Feis, "Between War and Peace; the Potsdam Conference" (Princeton University Press, 1960). Mr. Feis, as Special Consultant to three U. S. Secretaries of State, had firsthand knowledge of the events reported here, and his history, based on offical reports and records, is drawn upon, along with other published sources, throughout this book.

The facts of the Potsdam Conference itself and of the inter-allied discussions leading up to it show that (1) at no time did the Western Allies fail to state that the German-Polish settlement must await a peace treaty and (2) at no time did the Soviet Government fail to concede the point — or even, in some instances, to state the point voluntarily.

For example, during the Potsdam Conference, Stalin, on July 21, 1945, tried to defend the presence of Polish forces in Eastern Germany. He conceded that they were there by Soviet permission despite the protests of the American and British governments. But Stalin added that after all the boundaries were not yet settled. Moreover, although it was true, said Stalin, that "Polish administrators" were in the Soviet Zone of Germany, the western frontier question was open; the Soviet Union was not obligated.

"You are not?" asked President Truman, obviously wishing to get the point clearly on the record.

"No," replied Stalin.*

Unilateral Territorial Changes

Stalin may not have been "obligated", but in the Oder-Neisse area he and the Polish Communists certainly presented the Potsdam Conference with the crowning fait accompli in a whole series of unilateral actions taken under auspices of the Red Army in central Europe.

Contrary to the agreements made at Yalta to reserve the final settlement of the Polish borders to the peace conference, the Soviet Union had conveyed territorial sovereignty over the German East, with the exception of the area around Königsberg, to the Polish provisional government in Warsaw that was dependent on Moscow.

This unauthorized change in the map of Europe had occurred midway between Yalta and Potsdam: The Polish provisional regime

---

* Feis, op. cit.

acted on March 14, 1945 — even before the end of the war— to establish four voivodships or provinces in the area east of the Oder and the Western Neisse. This rejuggling of the map followed on March 20 by the announcement that the city of Danzig was the fifth Polish voivodship.

In other words, the Western Allies came to the Potsdam Conference, which was supposed to make provisional postwar settlements, faced with "postwar settlements" that had already been executed behind the fighting lines by the Communists.

Even before Potsdam it had become clear, of course, that the Western willingness to consider a "shifting of Poland to the west" had been used against the West and against, for that matter, the Polish people. While the Western Allies had gone to war to defeat a dictatorship, and had hoped to create a new Polish nation as a bulwark of democracy, their best efforts had helped — however unintentionally — to place Poland within the Soviet Bloc. Moreover, the Communist-manufactured German-Polish arrangement of 1945 extended Communist dictatorship not only to the Oder and the Western Neisse, but to the Elbe: to the heart of Europe.

At Potsdam, the Western Allies met with the Soviet representatives to do all that was possible to do about a situation in which two of the free world's major goals had — at least temporarily — been lost. The Communists had — at least temporarily — remade the map of central Europe. And they had denied Poland a democratic government that could work out honorable settlements with its neighbor Germany.

As Churchill recalls of the year 1945 in his "Triumph and Tragedy", the Western Allies "were as far as ever from any real and fair attempt to obtain the will of the Polish nation by free elections".

At this writing, that "will of the Polish nation by free elections" has still not been achieved. Until both the Germans as a whole are free to speak for themselves and until the Poles are at least free enough of Moscow's domination to negotiate honorably at a conference table, there seems no prospect of a fair and lasting settlement of the Oder-Neisse question, involving one of the most important frontiers in central Europe.

What the Western Allies could do at Potsdam, they did: They insisted that the way be left open for fair settlements in central Europe at a later date. Specifically, the Potsdam Agreement makes clear that

> "the final delimitation of the Western frontier of Poland *should await the peace settlement*"; that Germany's Eastern Territories were being placed "under the *administration* of the Polish state" and that

> the Oder-Neisse boundary was in effect "*pending the final determination* of Poland's western frontier".

Chapter 6:

THE ODER-NEISSE PROBLEM SINCE 1945

"Are mass expulsions crimes only when they are undertaken by our enemies in wartime, but justified means of social reorganization when our allies sponsor them in peacetime?"

Bertrand Russell

"Poland has neither the human nor the material means of digesting the German territory up to the Oder River. These territories are a gift fraught with danger. This can be only a temporary solution which will end on the day when Poland will have regained her liberty."

General Władysław Anders,
Polish military leader of World War II

As General Anders said, Poland may have lacked both the human and the material means to "digest" the Oder-Neisse area — but nobody can accuse her Communist regime of not having tried.

Even while the war was continuing, in March 1945 (see Chapter 4), the Soviet Government and the Red Army handed over German Eastern Territories to the Poles, and the areas, including Danzig, were promptly carved into five voivodships or provinces. Ever since the war, the Polish regime has tried to perpetuate this unilateral "settlement" of the German Polish question. She has done so by taking three measures:

1. Forceful evacuation of most of the German settlers, in a way that was not contemplated at Potsdam (and without the slightest resort even to such procedures as plebiscites, which were held in part of Central Europe after World War I);

2. Only partially successful attempts to resettle the area with Poles, Ukrainians and others;

3. Unsuccessful attempts to gain general international recognition for her series of faits accomplis in Central Europe.

The Polish regime's unilateral actions (supported when not initiated by the Soviet Government) since 1945 have flown in the face of the Potsdam Agreement, which stipulated that the Oder-Neisse Line is to be a provisional settlement pending a peace treaty. We have seen in earlier chapters that the arrangement can, in fact, be only a provisional settlement: both on grounds of international law and in consideration of the history of five, six and more centuries of European civilization.

In reviewing the disposition of German territory since 1945 by the Polish regime, it must be remembered, if one is to see the matter in perspective, that this Polish government was not chosen in free elections; nor, at this writing, has it yet been permitted even a relative degree of independence of the Soviet Union, as leader of the East Bloc. In fact, the extreme nature of some of the territorial claims put forward since 1945 by Poles indicates that the maneuvers have been primarily in the service, not of the Polish nation, but of Communist policy for Europe as a whole.

It is to be regretted that even Poles not under the influence of Soviet Communist policy — notably, exiled Polish statesmen — have often felt impelled to compete — to "keep up with the Joneses", as it were — by making similar exaggerated claims against Germany.

In Poland itself, ever since 1945, the regime's propaganda has maintained that the Oder-Neisse arrangement, instead of the provisional arrangement it was declared by the Allies to be, has been an award to Poland of "regained" territory.

The absurdity of the claim that the Oder-Neisse area is really a "regained" part of Poland was pointed up by a U. S. legislator, the late Rep. B. Carroll Reece of Tennessee. He suggested an imaginary parallel in America: "Suppose that the British Queen would this year set sail for Jamestown, Virginia, not to commemorate with us Americans the establishment in this hemisphere of the first colony of English-sepaking people, but, instead, to regain her crown colony because of a position of overlordship dating back to the late Middle Ages."

Nor were some Poles satisfied even with claiming the Oder-Neisse areas. A year after the Potsdam Agreement, the Polish Communist regime was demanding still more German territory than it already occupied. Its agent, F. Stojanowski, in 1946 demanded a Polish western boundary along the Elbe River in Central Germany. He asked for bridgeheads west of the Elbe at Hamburg, Magdeburg and Dresden. As a map prepared in 1947 by the Civil Administration Division of the U. S. Office of Military Government for Germany shows, the Polish — or at least the Communist — idea in 1946 was that Schleswig-Holstein, Mecklenburg and the northern part of Brandenburg were to be lumped together into an Elbe state, and the rest into a Lausitz state — both to form an integral part of a "Greater Poland".

The demand, to be sure, came to nothing. But it is recalled here for the light it throws on the attitude of the Moscow-dominated regime that has ruled in Warsaw since 1945. When that regime has solemnly demanded parts of Central Germany; when it continues to claim the German Eastern Territories of the Oder-Neisse area as "traditionally Polish", the question arises: Has Warsaw been serving the genuine interests of Poland, or has the regime up to this writing felt constrained to make claims in line with the expansionist tactics of Soviet Communism?

The Expulsions — and Their Significance Today

Article XII of the Potsdam Agreement of 1945 states that the three heads of government agree that, in regard to population movements in Central Europe, "any such transfer that will take place should be effected in an orderly and humane way".

Even earlier, before the war had ended, the Western Allies were confronted by flights and expulsions under conditions that were anything but humane. Moreover, Western acquiescence in what was happening was based to an important degree on partly misleading and partly untrue statements by Soviet representatives. For example, on February 7, 1945, Prime Minister Churchill said to Stalin: "I was conscious of a large body of opinion in Great Britain which was frankly shocked at the idea of moving millions of people by force". To which Stalin replied that "there were no Germans in these (East German) areas, as they had all run away".* The fact is that those Germans who had fled in the face of the advancing Red Army had no notion that they were to be prevented from returning to their homelands after the war. "The procedure of preventing the evacuated population of entire provinces to return after the close of hostilities was unknown in Europe before 1945. The return of 1,500,000 German refugees in May and June of 1945 from Czechoslovakia and the Russian Zone of Germany to the Oder-Neisse provinces, despite the threats of deportation, hunger and further humiliations, showed the attachment of the eastern Germans to their homeland."** They kept returning as long as they physically could do so. For example, in the early summer of 1945, not less than one million Silesians returned — even though the Polish militia had closed the bridges on the Neisse as early as June 1, 1945.***

Stalin indulged in further deceit during this same period by telling President Truman (echoing his earlier report to Churchill) that all the Germans had fled. The President was not taken in by the broad Soviet assertion; secretly, he believed that "the Russians had killed the German population or had chased them into our

---

* Churchill, "The Second World War", Vol VI.
** Zoltan Michael Szaz, "Germany's Eastern Frontiers" (Chicago, 1960), p. 96.
*** Ibid.

zones" — but he had no way of knowing that in fact more than four and one-half million Germans were still living in the Oder-Neisse areas.*

Within months, it had become clear enough what was happening by unilateral exertion of force. At Fulton, Missouri, on March 5, 1946, Prime Minister Churchill declared:

> "The Russian-dominated Polish government has been encouraged to make enormous and grievous inroads upon Germany, and mass expulsions of millions of Germans on a scale grievous and undreamed of are now taking place."**

It is not the purpose of this book to chronicle once more what Churchill called the "grievous" record. Suffice it to say here that the expulsions separated countless families and took the lives of between two and three million people.

If that seems sparse comment on a tragic era, the Germans are well aware that the tragedy of the expulsions followed on the heels of a previous tragic era — in which the acts of a German dictatorship resulted in death for many more millions of people, in Germany and throughout the world.

Moreover, there is no need, for the purpose of our presentation, to detail the almost unbelievable story of the cruel trek across central Europe. For those who wish to inform themeslves of it, there is ample documentation elsewhere.

Two points about the mass expulsions, however, remain pertinent to the German-Polish problem as it still exists today:

> The manner in which the "transfers" were carried out was a further violation of the letter and spirit of the Potsdam Agreement;

> The expulsions, far from ending German concern over the Eastern Territories, have served to make the matter a living issue for the entire German population (see Chapter 8).

* Harry S. Truman, "Memoirs", Vol I, p. 369.
** The New York Times, March 6, 1946.

Are the Expellees "Dying Out"?

Many persons who concede that the expulsion of Germans from their homes was both inhuman and of highly questionble legality are apt nevertheless to add: "But all this is history now — and the expulsions at least solved a problem." The truth is that *the expulsions did not solve a problem, but created one: They have elevated the events in Germany's Eastern Territories from a regional to a national concern.*

The international press has reported in detail the annual meetings of expellees — and thus has indirectly allowed the impression to be created that the only Germans who are concerned with the Oder-Neisse problem are an aging generation of men and women who once lived in the Eastern Territories. Justice for these millions would be worth some international concern for its own sake. But the significance of the mass expulsions extends beyond the expellees' own lifetimes. Not only their children and children's children, but to a greater or lesser extent all Germans are becoming acutely aware of the temporarily "lost territories" in the East. It would not be considered chauvinism if citizens of Great Britain, the United States or the Soviet Union were to keep in mind the loss of one-fifth of their territory. No more is it chauvinism for Germans to remember.

As we shall see in Chapter 8, the Oder-Neisse problem is very much alive. It concerns *not the expellees alone but Germans in general.* For the Eastern Territories are a culturally, economically and historically important part of Germany within her legitimate national borders. It would be hard to find an example in history of a people's acquiescing permanently to the amputation of a comparable part of its homeland.

This circumstance — the fact of Poland's unilateral "solution" of the Oder-Neisse problem, under Soviet Communist auspices — has created not a dying, but a living and a growing problem for Germans and for the international community of nations.

82

This book concerns itself with Polish domestic politics only as those politics bear on the German-Polish problem in Central Europe. One of these aspects of postwar events in Poland constitutes, as we have noted, another violation of Allied agreements: The Poles have not been granted a chance to form a genuinely representative government. This statement is pertinent to a discussion of the Oder-Neisse problem, because it bears directly on Allied intentions and promises. The unilateral action of the regime now in power in Poland, in trying to fix to its advantage the German-Polish border, has no authorization stemming from the intention of the Allies expressed during and after the second World War. For this was one of the circumstances within which even a *temporary* Polish *administration* of the German lands was to be countenanced: that a democratic Poland would arise as Germany's neighbor.

The Yalta Conference of February 1945 is quite specific on the point. The three Heads of Government — U. S., British and Soviet — outlined the ways by which the Polish provisional government that had been formed, as we have seen, by disciples of Moscow, was to be reorganized so as to qualify for recognition by the United States and Great Britain. The formula states:

> "The Provisional Government which is now functioning in Poland should ... be reorganized on a broader democratic basis with the inclusion of democratic leaders from Poland itself and from Poles abroad."

The same declaration laid down the provision that this reorganized government

> "shall be pledged to the holding of free and unfettered elections as soon as possible on the basis of universal suffrage and secret ballot".

However, Stalin's brand of Communism was in the saddle throughout Eastern Europe, and the pledge was not kept.

On the contrary, the Communist take-over in Poland that had begun even before the war's end was completed shortly after the war. Open breaches of pledges made to the Allies began occurring only a year after the creation of Poland's so-called "government of national unity". Government authorities falsified the returns for the abolition of the Polish Senate in the three-point referendum of June 30, 1946. U. S. Ambassador Lane protested to the government:

> "The method used in tabulating the ballots and reporting the vote has given rise to charges of serious irregularities, including the removal of the ballot boxes from polling places in contravention of the referendum law..." *

Communist seizure of the nation that the Western Allies thought they were re-creating as a democracy was completed with "elections" in January 1947. Premier Osóbka-Morawski was succeeded by Josef Cyrankiewicz the Polish Peasant Party was dissolved, and Vice Premier Mikołajczyk was forced to flee.**

The Communists have continued in power in Poland from that day to this. Insofar as they have claimed as their own Germany's Eastern Territories, they have sought to advance to the heart of Europe the sphere controlled by the Communist Bloc. Thus the Oder-Neisse situation is backed only by the might of the Red Army, not by international law — and least of all by Allied intentions and pledges.

The Polish-Russian Frontier

During the same year, 1945, in which Polish Communists with the support of the Red Army were taking over the German Eastern Territories, Moscow moved to "legalize" her gains at Poland's expense in the east. We have seen (Chapter 4) that Poland took

---

* Arthur Bliss Lane, "I Saw Poland Betrayed" (Indianapolis, 1948), p. 262.
** Statistical Yearbook of Poland 1947, pp 47—52.

84

over areas from the Soviet Union in the Peace of Riga of 1921. On August 17, 1945, a Polish-Soviet agreement was signed in Moscow, returning these areas to Russia and establishing the new frontier more or less along the so-called Curzon Line. The agreement took effect on February 5, 1946.

This settlement in the east doubtless increased the determination of the Polish regime to try to "legalize" its acquisition of German areas in the west. It remains for the objective observer, however, to decide for himself whether any Nation A (Poland), by surrendering territory to any Nation B (the U. S. S. R.), gains a legal, moral, political or ethnological right to take territory from any Nation C (Germany).

The Görlitz "Agreement" of 1950

The Polish regime knew that any attempt at international "recognition" of the Oder-Neisse Line as the Polish-German frontier would stand on extremely unfirm ground. For one thing, the Western Allies had never ceased to remind the world that the Potsdam agreements were provisional — as indeed they perforce had to be, pending the formation of a German government empowered to negotiate its own frontiers at a peace treaty.

Thus, in the words of President Truman, "cession of territory was subject to the peace treaty" and the Western Allies had authorized "only the temporary administration of the area" by Poland.*

The Polish regime, however, preferred some sort of on-paper statement to none at all — even if the agreement must be concluded with a regime not empowered to speak for the German people: namely, the regime set up under Communist control in the Soviet-occupied zone of Germany.

* Harry S. Truman, "Memoirs", Vol I, p. 405.

This Communist puppet regime within Central Germany (i) has never held free elections (ii) is not recognized as the rightful authority by the mass of the Germans themselves (iii) enjoys practically no international recognition, least of all by the free nations and (iv) in any case has as its subjects only 16 million Germans, compared with the more than 53 million Germans who live in freedom in the Federal Republic of Germany, west of the Iron Curtain. It was this German Communist splinter regime, which calls itself the "German Democratic Republic" or "DDR", that concluded an "agreement" with the Polish Communist regime at Görlitz on June 6, 1950, declaring the Oder-Neisse to be the final boundary between Germany and Poland.

The Görlitz "agreement", whatever it may have done for morale within the Communist Bloc, only served to dramatize to the world the illegality of the Oder-Neisse settlement. Protests against and disavowals of the legality of the settlement were quick to come from free Germany and from the Western powers.

In a note, the Federal Government (West Germany) protested the Görlitz agreement, and observed that the boundaries of Germany could not be changed, except by a peace treaty concluded with the whole of Germany.

This note was handed by the three Western High Commissioners for Germany to the Soviet commander in chief in Germany, General Chuikov. In transmitting the note, the Western spokesmen emphasized on their own that the German boundaries, according to the agreement reached at Potsdam, could not be finally determined until a peace treaty was signed.

The French: "No"

In Paris on July 7, 1950, a government statement was issued as follows: "The French Foreign Ministry authorizes its High Commissioner in Germany to state that France explicitly recognizes as German State territory the area within the frontiers of 1937 and that the Federal Government as a result of free elections is regarded as the spokesman for the whole of Germany." *

The British: "No"

On the same day, the following government statement was issued in London: "The Oder-Neisse line had never been decided upon as a final boundary ... The British point of view has not changed since Potsdam. Stalin himself had stated on July 21, 1945, that the final settlement of the western Polish boundary could not be undertaken before a peace treaty was concluded ... The British Government therefore intended to ignore the Görlitz agreement and to regard it as nonexistent."

The Americans: "No"

On the following day, July 8, 1950, the U. S. Department of State joined in the stand of its allies: "The present Soviet Zone regime ... is not ... entitled to speak for the German people. The United States Government has in the past never recognized the Oder-Neisse line as the final eastern frontier of Germany. It does not recognize the present arrangement arrived at by the Polish Government and the administration of Eastern Germany."

The Germans: "No"

And on July 9, 1950, the German Federal Government followed up its earlier protest with a statement as follows: "The so-called government of the Soviet Zone has no right whatsoever to speak for the German people. Its arrangements and agreements are null and void. The decision on the eastern German territories at present under Polish and Soviet administration cannot and will not be

---

* France had associated herself with Potsdam Agreement, joining the U. S., the U. K. and the U.S.S.R. as the fourth contracting Power, on August 4, 1945.

taken until a peace treaty is concluded with a united Germany. The German Federal Government, as the spokesman for the entire German nation, will never accept the annexation, contrary to every principle of law and humanity, of these purely German territories. The Federal Government will seek a just solution of this question in future peace negotiations between ... Poland and a democratic, united Germany."

A Dictated Boundary

To thoughtful Poles who realize that their foreign policy since 1945 has not been one of their own choosing, one of the greatest ironies of the situation in which their country finds itself is symbolized by the above-mentioned Görlitz agreement of 1950. The present frontier between the Polish people and the German people is a result not of popular will but of Communist power politics. The Oder-Neisse boundary was created by a totalitarian policy, and to this day it is "recognized" only by totalitarian regimes. Among Poland's western neighbors, the Oder-Neisse line has been "recognized" as permanent only by a regime that rules the one part of Germany that is as unfree as were all the Germans under Hitler. In the west, Germany's boundaries unite her with her neighbors; in the east, the dictated Oder-Neisse line divides Poles from Germans — and Europe from Europe.

The Uneasiness of New Settlers

Against this post-1945 background, it is not surprising that many of the Poles and others who were resettled in the Oder-Neisse areas since the war have not sunk roots there. Many of them lack the feeling of having attained a new home. Their realization — despite their regime's propaganda blasts — that the area where they are living is a focal point of Polish-German disagreement is largely responsible. There has been an abnormally strong fluctuation of population in the Oder-Neisse area. Many of the resettled persons have decided at some time since 1945 that it was the better part of wisdom not to stay, but to create a new existence for themselves in Poland proper, that is, in the Polish territory east of the border of the former German Reich. Naturally this insecurity — which stems from a deep sense of reality and the rightness of things — has impaired economic reconstruction in the German Eastern Territories now under Polish administration.

Yet it is not the fault of the persons now living in Germany's Eastern Territories that a maneuver of power politics has placed them there. As Chapter 9 observes in more detail, these people need have no fear for their future once a fair German-Polish settlement of the status of the area has been negotiated.

An Artificial Situation

The statement by the Polish General Anders quoted at the beginning of this chapter — that "Poland has neither the human nor the material means of digesting the German territory up to the Oder River" — has proved true since 1945. Ample criticisms of what has happened in the German Eastern Territories under Polish rule are at hand, from Polish sources. *

Such criticisms, and Warsaw's realization that its artificial resettlement policy was falling short of its goals, led to creation of what the Polish regime called the Society for the Recovered Territories. A commission of this group investigated the situation in the Oder-Neisse area, then reported in guarded but highly significant language that in these German areas under Polish control: "Positive and negative phenomena neutralize each other, while before the undertaking of the travel for study purposes, it was assumed that positive phenomena in the political, economic and social life of the provinces would prevail." **

---

* Accounts from the Polish press are available, for example, in the archives of the Göttinger Arbeitskreis, and, in collected form, in „Die deutschen Ostgebiete jenseits von Oder und Neisse im Spiegel der polnischen Presse" (Holzner, Würzburg 1958).

** Report as reproduced in Expellee Press Service, German version (31), 1957.

The "negative" phenomena uncovered in the Polish investigation included a variety of political, economic and social problems. One of the difficulties was found to be a general lack of initiative on the part of the Poles, Ukrainians and others who have moved or have been moved to the Oder-Neisse area by the Polish regime. Many persons, as noted above, have refused to stay. Moreover:

> "Rumors and whisperings prevail and cause a certain feeling of insecurity in the provinces among the population, which still fears eventual reattachment to Germany."*

As an American observer** described the situation: "In much the same way as in the 1940s the misled ethnic Germans felt unhappy over holding what they learned was stolen property ... so these Poles and Ukrainians learned that they were settled on stolen property ... Unspoiled people seem to have an innate sense of distinguishing between right and wrong."

But it is far from the intentions of German expellees and of responsible persons generally in the Federal Republic of Germany to compound wrong with new wrong in central Europe. The Germans have renounced revenge, including solutions by force, and have voluntarily pledged that there will be no new expulsions. Indeed, as Chapter 9 points out, the Oder-Neisse territories have room and resources for everybody who wants to make a productive living there.

The current uneasiness over the Oder-Neisse situation, therefore, is the uneasiness that inevitably accompanies dictated "solutions" to human and political problems. Increasingly the world is becoming aware — and the awareness is spreading among peoples on both sides of the Iron Curtain — that the Oder-Neisse arrangement must be replaced by a fair settlement based on negotiations.

---

* Ibid. English wordings is from Szaz, op. cit., p. 145.
** Rep. Reece, op. cit.

Chapter 7:

POLISH MISGIVINGS

"It is difficult to credit with good faith any person who asserts that Poland's western boundary was fixed by the conferees (at Potsdam in 1945) or that there was a promise that it would be established at some particular place."

> James F. Byrnes
> Former U. S. Secretary of State

"... national consciousness is stronger and more durable than governments."

> Ignace Paderewski
> Former Prime Minister of Poland

It has been the fate of modern Poland to go too far — or to be pushed into going too far. We have seen (Chapter 5) that Moscow was instrumental in arranging the Oder-Neisse Line at the end of the second world war — a line deep in German territory. Something quite similar has happened before, in the memory of many living persons. Early in April 1919, U. S. President Woodrow Wilson commented acidly on a policy of "weakening Germany by *giving Poland territory to which she has no right.*"* (See also Chapter 4.)

The renowned former Prime Minister of the Union of South Africa, General Jan C. Smuts, saw the same danger. On May 22,

* R. S. Baker, "Woodrow Wilson and World Settlement", Vol. II, p. 60.

1919, he wrote to the British Prime Minister, Lloyd George, regarding the Polish settlement contained in the Versailles Treaty: "I think the two cardinal errors in policy of this treaty are the long occupation of the Rhineland and *the enlargement of Poland beyond anything which we had contemplated during the war.*" He added: "These two errors are full of menace for the future peace of Europe ..."*

Polish Misgivings

Such warnings to Poland from abroad have been echoed in more recent times by thoughtful Poles. At the time of his resignation of July 6, 1945, the Polish Ambassador in Washington, Jan Ciechanowski, asked: "How can one explain to the Polish nation that their country is but a home on wheels to be pushed eastward and westward as may suit the imperialist aims of its mighty neighbors *in defiance of the principle of self-determination of peoples for which they fought?* Some day, answers to these questions will have to be found if justice is to survive."

And General Władysław Anders, the well-known Polish military leader in the second world war, declared in an interview on December 14, 1946: "*Poland has neither the human nor the material means of digesting the German territory up to the Oder River .. We do not want anything to which we are not entitled ...*"

Allied Warnings

Well over a year earlier, the Western Allies sounded the same warning. Here, for example, is a report by historian Herbert Feis, who has been quoted previously in this book, on the British attitude at Potsdam in 1945:

"*Churchill was not to be quieted. Polish territorial claims were immoderate. What was asked would not even be good for Poland.*" **

* Ibid., Vol. III. p. 461.
** Feis, op. cit.

92

Sir Winston Churchill also recalls for himself in "Triumph and Tragedy" what happened in the summer of 1945 in Potsdam. Polish representatives had been summoned there for consultations. In the afternoon of July 24 the Poles called on the British Prime Minister, who received them in the company of Anthony Eden, Clark Kerr and Sir Harold Alexander. The area that the Poles (under Soviet Russian encouragement) were preparing to absorb, Churchill told them, would deprive Germany of one-quarter of its arable land and would cause a forced migration of eight or nine million people. In Churchill's words:

"We ... were convinced that it was just as dangerous for the Poles to press too far to the west as they had once pressed too far to the east."

Voices of Moderation Ignored

Unfortunately, with Communist tactics ruling Eastern Europe, Allied and Polish voices of moderation were largely silenced. It is symptomatic that, as we have seen (Chapter 6), in 1946 there were Polish agents who wanted Poland to expand still farther west than even the Oder-Neisse Line. They were rebuffed; but in claiming as its own the Oder-Neisse area, the Polish Communist regime continues to hold what General Anders was frank to call land "to which we are not entitled".

As long as a Communist puppet regime in Poland claims German territory for Poland, some Polish politicians abroad seem to find it hard to refrain from claiming less. But they might ask themselves whether this policy is statesmanlike. For history — supported by Polish and non-Polish voices like those quoted in this chapter — demonstrates that only fair play between neighbors can in the long run be good politics.

Every Pole who realizes that right is ultimately more powerful than might is bound to feel uneasy about the present Oder-Neisse arrangement.

Indeed, Poles need not have very long memories to recall the havoc that has been created in central Europe in the past by unfair violations of legitimate national interests. Where Poland is concerned, her most distinguished representatives have always been quick to proclaim that dictated territorial changes can never lead to good-neighborly relations. Ignace Paderewski, Poland's then Minister President, voiced just such a warning in 1919. It is true that he was not warning against the handing over of parts of Germany (Chapter 4) to the new Polish republic; he was indignant, rather, at the assignment of the Teschen part of Silesia to Czechoslovakia, to the disadvantage of Poland. When the ambassadors' conference at Spa had made its decision, Paderewski wrote to Millerand:

> "*The plain fact of the matter is that the decision of the ambassadors' conference has torn open an abyss between the two nations (Poland and Czechoslovakia), an abyss that nothing can fill ... The Polish government has signed a formal obligation which must now be carried through. It will however never be able to convince the Polish nation that justice has been satisfied. The national consciousness is stronger and more durable than governments.*"

To repeat Paderewski: "... national consciousness is stronger and more durable than governments." Should he not have been aware, we may ask in hindsight, that in regard to "national consciousness", the German people were not less sensitive than the Polish? That the denial to the Germans of the right of self-determination under the Versailles Treaty would inevitably risk fatal consequences?

For the German-Polish situation between the two world wars was one of the favorite targets of Hitler's propaganda. In the soil of an offended sense of national consciousness and justice were sown the dragon's seed of hatred and revenge.

Fortunately, nationalism is definitely not the predominating spirit in the free part of Europe today. Western Europeans are learning to settle their differences by negotiating. Then why recite the above instances of past wrongs? In order to underline the danger of perpetuating injustices in Central Europe, where negotiations between equal partners have *not* yet become self-understood.

Poles as well as Germans have known enough suffering in modern times from infringements of each other's sovereignty. They can take a new course. Their common frontier can be negotiated. Either a national or an international status for the territory under discussion can also be negotiated (see Chapter 10).

But in any event, Poles who remember the past must surely be as convinced as Germans that in Europe's future there will be no place for unilateral settlements of matters that concern two nations; dictation is going out of style.

An Element in Poland's Bondage

The Poles have devoted much of their past existence to the pursuit of national freedom. The possession of the Oder-Neisse territories on an illegal basis through unilateral action is one of the factors that strengthens the chains of their bondage. Evidences are strong that the Communist tacticians in Moscow planned it that way. As a U. S. legislator* has put the case:

"The present illegal occupation by the Poles of German soil and property — so the Kremlin schemed — would chain Poland safely to the Kremlin walls; because only with Soviet military support can Poland hope to hold on to the German provinces while, on the other hand, the bridges between the German and the Polish people would be out of commission as long as the wrong continues."

* Rep. B. Carroll Reece of Tennessee in the House of Representatives, May 16, 1957. See complete reference in footnote, Chapter 1.

95

The Kremlin's trap was clearly seen by a Polish historian, Oskar Halecki, who warned * in connection with the postwar provisional arrangement:

> "*The same people who now urge the Poles to accept the Russian offer will blame them in the future for having created, through their imperialism, a new problem which will trouble the peace of Europe.*"

Along the same lines, Roman Umiastowski, the Polish author, declared immediately after the war:

> "*The Kremlin's proposal of compensation was not so much in order to justify the Russian annexation of eastern Poland as to extend their (Soviet) rule to the banks of the Oder.*" **

The "Polish Vote" Abroad

Much has been said and written about the "political impracticability" of causing possible offense to Poles who reside and vote in various Western lands, notably Great Britain and America. The "Polish vote" is often alluded to — in its literal and figurative sense — as a ground not to "do anything about the Oder-Neisse situation" that would be displeasing to Poles living away from Poland.

* "The Review of Politics" (University of Notre Dame), April 1945, April 1946.
** "Poland, Russia and Great Britain, 1941—1945" (London, 1946).

Immanuel Kant
(born at Königsberg 1724, died there 1804). The German philosopher sought to harmonize earlier British philosophic trends. He gave the world his famed essay "on perpetual peace". In 1946 the U. S. S. R. renamed his home city Kaliningrad.

Sand Dunes, Sea and Memories

This picturesque stretch of the Baltic is known as the Frische Nehrung. The tongue of land above separates the sea's rolling surf from the bay called the Frische Haff. Millions of Germans and tens of thousands of their guests have memories of this idyllically quiet vacation land where land, sea and sky meet. After the area was placed under Polish administration in 1945, the world-known bird sanctuary at Rossitten was re-established in the western part of Germany. Most famous of the bathing resorts on the Frische Nehrung was Kahlberg.

As early as Potsdam in 1945, however, President Truman, considering the so-called "Polish vote", recognized that there was something much more basic than a frontier that would influence it: *the question of freedom for Poland.*

Truman told Stalin:

"There are six million Poles in the United States. A free election reported to the United States by a free press would make it much easier to deal with these Polish people."

At the time, Prime Minister Churchill also clearly put the situation of freedom-loving Poles. He recounted what the Polish and British nations had gone through together. He recalled how the British had given a home to Poles who had fled from Hitler's invasion. He wanted the Poles abroad treated in a way that they and the world would approve. Stalin uttered a hearty "Of course".* The Russian added that "The British had the same objectives as the Soviets. They asked... that Poland be made an attractive place for the Poles to return to."

Poles at home and abroad can best decide for themselves to what degree the spirit and the letter of that inter-Allied conversation at Potsdam has been implemented in deed. Whether or not Poles abroad consider Poland "an attractive place to return to", it is clear that there has been no "free election reported... by a free press" in postwar Poland. Yet precisely that domestic freedom was the condition (Chapter 5) which was set in connection with the provisional arrangement of the Oder-Neisse situation.

Poles in Exile and Poles at Home

It is not within the scope of this book to weigh the various political stands of rival Polish statesmen at home and abroad. But a significant and encouraging fact is emerging: It seems clear that Poles of all persuasions yearn for more freedom than they now

---

* Feis, op. cit.

possess. Even with agreement on the political definition of "freedom" left unsettled among them, one common denominator of this desired freedom is *the freedom to resume traditional ties with the rest of Europe.* Poles who maintain ties with Moscow and Poles who do not are alike in wanting — secretly, and often, these days, openly — more freedom to determine at least the basic elements of their foreign relations for themselves. *Most Poles want their nation's future destiny to be linked with that of Europe, both east and west.*

As recently as the year 1961, a journal published by Poles in London* declared that there is a "deeply-rooted ailment" which is only to be cured by "a thorough-going reconstruction of Europe". The journal noted with approval President Kennedy's statement earlier that year that negotiations with the Soviet Union would be fruitful "if the Soviet Union accepts for Berlin — indeed, for all Europe — the principle of self-determination which it proclaims in other parts of the world."

As for the Poles in Poland, they too are eager for more national independence — quite aside from the question of continued closeness to Moscow. As recently as late in 1961 the international press was reporting restlessness and desire for elemental reforms in Poland:

> "... the Poles have been asking the most fundamental questions and making the most basic demands for reform yet voiced anywhere in the Communist camp."**

To repeat, it is not within the intention of this book to consider, as such, what must of course in the end be a Polish decision: the constitution of Poland's government. However, one of the tests of the good intentions of *any* Polish government certainly will be its *willingness to negotiate* with its neighbors over common problems and common opportunities. One of the tests of the independence of such a government, moreover, will be its *ability to enter into such negotiations.* And there is no factor more basic to the future of

---

* "Polish Affairs", July/August 1961.
** The New York Times, international edition, Dec. 5, 1961.

98

Europe (aside from such ultimate issues as self-determination itself) than the task of negotiating a fair basis for Polish-German relations.

A Polish Dilemma

Meanwhile, judging by what Poles say in lands where they are granted freedom of speech, many of them are presently involved in a dilemma — a sort of ideological self-contradiction. They want what they call a fair settlement in Central Europe — for Poland, but not necessarily for its neighbor, Germany. They speak of freedom for Poland, but not necessarily of freedom for the part of Germany that remains unfree. They oppose the Communist regime in their homeland, or at least they oppose its degree of non-freedom. Yet they ask the free world to recognize one of the major acts of that very regime which they criticize as being unfree: its annexation, with the backing of Moscow and the Red Army (Chapter 5), of German territory. In the same breath in which they condemn this or that "dictated" circumstance at home in Poland, they demand acceptance of a dictated frontier — a line that has been fixed by the free will of neither of the peoples whom it divides!

Their dilemma was foreseen by farsighted Poles long before the second world war ended. This was the warning of the Polish exile government in 1943:

> " . . . even though the Soviet government should, in compensation, support Polish claims to some German territories in the West, these new frontiers would make Poland dependent on her eastern neighbor, and enable the Soviet Union to use her as a springboard for extending its domination over Central Europe and Germany in particular." *

---

* Report of memorandum of Oct. 8, 1943, from the Polish Ambassador in London to the American Secretary of State. Cited in Herbert Feis, "Roosevelt, Churchill, Stalin: The War They Waged and the Peace They Sought" (Princeton University Press, 1957).

A Way Out of the Dilemma

There is a way for Poles to liberate themselves — short of war — from the present situation, a situation which Poles admit makes their nation "dependent on her eastern neighbor." While keeping normal ties with the Soviet Union, they can move toward normal ties with their other neighbors, both east and west. First of those neighbors to the west is Germany.

During 1963, at least two small, first steps were taken in the direction of that seemingly distant goal, Polish-German reconciliation:

1. German reporters and television teams were treated hospitably by the Polish regime — and in turn brought back to the Federal Republic of Germany an objective picture of life and aspirations in Poland today. In fact, some of the television films were so favorable that parts of German public opinion asked: Would the Poles be as fair in representing today's Germans?

2. Trade missions were set up by Bonn and Warsaw. Where trade exists, there is soil for other contacts to take root. As U. S. Secretary of State Dean Rusk put the case in Frankfurt during late 1963: "Trade and contacts with the Communist nations may help."

Chancellor Ludwig Erhard, moreover, has said that the Federal Republic of Germany under his charge "will devote its full attention to the improvement of the relations" between Germany and Eastern European states, including Poland. The Chancellor favors both "economic exchanges" and "cultural contacts" with Warsaw.

Again, let us quote a Polish source on the way out of this Polish dilemma. "Berlin, Germany and the Interests of Poland" is the heading of a recent article by the editor-in-chief of a newspaper published in London for Poles in exile (and by one means or another followed also by many Poles at home). The article states:

> *"The reality is that as long as Germany is divided into a Federal Republic and a Soviet Zone, Poland cannot figure*

*on a restoration of her independence. A perpetuation of the
partitioning of Germany signifies the perpetuation of the
partitioning of Europe into a free and an unfree Europe.
Paradoxical as it sounds, who knows whether we Poles don't
have an even greater interest in the reunification of Germany
than the Germans do themselves! From the Polish standpoint
there is no greater danger than the consolidation of the
present situation in Europe and Europe's partitioning. And
that fact must determine our attitude towards the question
of German unity." **

A Pole advocating Polish reconciliation one day with a reunited
Germany? Many Poles whose minds still look backward might he-
sitate over this idea. Particularly in the wake of invasion and war,
reconciliation comes slowly. But governmental systems change, peoples learn, and reconciliation comes.

Nobody expects men to reckon as coolly as electronic computers,
or to forgive as readily as saints. Yet even a minimum of clear
thinking about the matter, and even a minimum of good will about
the future will serve the purposes here: will enable farsighted
Poles to see the long-range wisdom of the passage quoted above
from a Polish newspaper.

Certainly there is much in the past for which the Germans must
seek to atone. There is much that gives Poles grounds for suspicion.
Yet the past *is* past. It is a past that will never be forgotten, but
also will never return — if only because the aggressive German
dictatorship victimized the German people as it victimized the
Poles.

The present in the free part of Germany is as different from
the past under dictatorship as day is from night. Poles need not
take the word of Germans for this; they have the testimony and
experience of many peoples of the West to go by: peoples who,
like the Poles, suffered from and fought a German dictatorship;

---

* "Dziennik Polski". Excerpt reprinted in "The English Bulletin", Bonn
Oct. 10, 1961.

peoples who are working and prospering with the new, democratic Federal Republic of Germany, as its friends and allies.

Some day Germany will be reunited, as Poland too, despite her partitions, has always won unity. Thoughtful Poles know that a final Polish-German settlement must await that day.

It is no insult or threat to the Soviet Union to state here an obvious truth: *Poland can "return to Europe" on the day when it is free to deal honorably with its neighbors both east and west.*

The currently existing arrangements affecting the Polish and the German peoples, chief among them the enforced Oder-Neisse settlement that is not a settlement, are bound to go. For these arrangements divide two peoples that history and geography have created as neighbors.

Chapter 8:

WHY ALL GERMANS AGREE

"Every person has a right to an ancestral home, and it is unjust to drive him from it if he has not made himself unworthy through his own guilt."

Pope Pius XII, 1948

"... this right to their native soil is an expression of the right of self-determination for others, and we shall always claim it passionately for ourselves."

Heinrich von Brentano
Former Federal Foreign Minister

The first quotation above illustrates a specific aspect of the German-Polish problem; the second, the problem as a whole. Pope Pius XII refers to the men, women and children who were driven out of their ancestral homelands behind the Oder and the Western Neisse Rivers (Chapter 6). The second quotation above, from a former German Foreign Minister, presents the matter of the German-Polish border as a problem that "passionately" concerns the whole German people.

The expellees as such have earned world attention and sympathy. As will be shown below, they have also earned criticism as alleged or potential disturbers of the peace. Neither attitude, sympathy for or distrust of the expellees, is an illuminating approach to the Oder-Neisse problem. It would be inaccurate to assume that Germany's claim for a fair, negotiated settlement of the status of her Eastern Territories is motivated by any demands of the expellees as a special-interest group. The expellees themselves see the issue not as "their" problem but as an all-German matter.

To be sure, it was these expellees, men, women and children not personally or collectively guilty of Hitler's war, who were present to witness the amputation of the easternmost part of the German nation. In the years since 1945, however, all Germany has come to experience the shock of the amputation. It is in reflection of this national development that Former Foreign Minister Brentano speaks of a right for "ourselves" — for all the German people.

This chapter seeks to throw light on why the Oder-Neisse problem concerns all the Germans. It explains why the status of the Eastern Territories will — inevitably — trouble not only the expellees but the Germans in general until the day the problem is settled. It will indicate that time alone (without negotiations between the Polish people and a free, united German people) cannot be expected to solve this key problem of Central Europe. These pages, too, will seek to remind the reader that any such simple "fading away" of the problem would be contradictory to the historical experiences of the world's national communities.

What Do the Expellees Want?

But first, what of the expellees as a group? Are they seeking to motivate their fellow Germans to join them in taking some precipitate or hard-and-fast action? Inasmuch as the expellees were the most immediate victims of Soviet Communist expansion, is this section of the German population bitter and set on revenge? In other words, are they as a group a danger to the peace of Europe?

"Hysterical" and "revanchist" are two among a myriad of trite labels that have been applied by Communist propagandists and by sensation-seeking journalists to the expellees from Germany's Eastern Territories. The reader can consult the official Charter of the German Expellees and decide for himself whether such terms apply. The Charter's first two articles follow:*

> "1. We, the expellees, renounce all thought of revenge and retaliation. Our resolution is a solemn and sacred one, in memory of the infinite suffering brought upon mankind, particularly during the past decade." (The Charter was published in 1950.)

> "2. We shall support with all our strength every endeavor directed towards the establishment of a united Europe, in which the nations may live in freedom from fear and coercion."

Thus the Charter begins by recognizing the "infinite suffering" that the Hitler dictatorship and Stalinist postwar power politics visited on Europe and the world. It looks forward to another kind of future. There is implicit in the above-quoted Article 2 a willingness, even an eagerness, "to support with all our strength" a fair, internationally negotiated solution in Central Europe. (See Chapter 9.)

On only one thing do the expellees insist — and not "hysterically" or "revanchistically" but rather in the spirit of the quotation from Pope Pius XII at the start of this chapter. The appropriateness and fairness of this one demand of the expellees the reader can also judge for himself; it too appears in the Expellees' Charter:

> "We have lost our homeland . . . To separate a man from his native land by force means to kill his soul."
> "We have suffered and experienced this fate."
> "We therefore feel competent to demand that the right to a homeland be recognized and be realized, as one of the basic rights of man . . ."

Fair Play as a Bulwark of German Democratic Forces

So much for the expellees. If they have been reasonable and patient in awaiting a peaceful solution of the Polish-German

* Full text in Appendix to this book.

border problem, it follows that every other element of the German population has been at least equally patient.

Yet is it wise to mortgage the future of democracy in Germany with a heritage of wrongs from the postwar era? Not only Germans have posed this question. As early as 1947, the Americans were aware of the importance to Europe of fair play in Germany. The official American standpoint, outlined by the U. S. delegation at the Moscow Conference of Foreign Ministers in that year, has remained a guideline of American policy. The U. S. position presented at the Moscow Conference was that a Polish-German settlement "should not discredit the democratic forces in Germany" and should not "give militant nationalist groups the chance to gain a hold on another generation of German youth".[*]

Democratic forces, in all the years since 1947, have not been discredited, nor have "militant nationalist groups" yet arisen to plague the young Federal Republic. But at the same time, the unsolved border problem with Poland has come to have, as part of the general unsolved problem of German unity, a growing hold on the minds of Germans.

Ever since the birth of the Federal Republic, Germany's reunification and a fair, negotiated settlement of the problem of the Eastern Territories have been the concern of the people and of their government.

Germany's Intentions

A statement of July 9, 1950, by the Government of the Federal Republic of Germany declared:

> "The decision on the eastern German territories at present under Polish and Soviet administration cannot and will not be taken until a peace treaty is concluded with a united Germany. The German Federal Government, as the spokesman

---

[*] U. S. Department of State Bulletin, April 20, 1947, p. 694.

for the entire German nation, will never accept the annexation,
contrary to every principle of law and humanity, of these
purely German territories. The Federal Government will seek
a just solution of this question in future peace negotiations
between a genuinely democratic Poland and a democratic,
united Germany."

This has continued to be the stand of the German Government,
the parliament and the people. Our present chapter indicates why
there is such unanimity within free Germany on the Polish-German
problem; and why that stand has continued to merit the support
of Germany's allies and the sympathy of free peoples everywhere.

Why Time Alone Is No Remedy

A common fallacy has been to assume that "the Oder-Neisse
problem will solve itself as the expellees from the German Eastern
Territories die out". There are two errors in this assumption.

First, it overlooks the fact that the expellees have children, and
that there will be the children's children. Not long ago, a German
public-opinion poll established that a majority of the expellees
"has the firm desire to return to the country they left in 1945,
a small minority is yet undecided and a negligible fraction wants
to stay where they are today".

Second, the fallacious idea that time will solve the Oder-Neisse
problem also overlooks the fact that the problem affects not only
the expellees but the German people as a whole. It is safe to assume
that millions of Germans who did not personally suffer from the
events since 1945 in the Eastern Territories have been made aware
of the German-Polish problem by those events.

The westward trek of the expellees after 1945 brought with it
a consciousness of injustice that has long since become the common
consciousness of the whole German people. This is not simply a
German phenomenon: It is a fact of history that a lost homeland
burns in memory. Examples in the west are Alsace-Lorraine (France)

and the Saar (Germany). The East provides a still more pertinent example: The Polish people's steadfastness in enduring, then overcoming, the various partitions of the Polish homeland is here the most appropriate illustration of this truth that history teaches.

Facing the Past

In the first hard years after the war, it is true, the typical German family had other things to do than to think constantly of the partition of the German homeland. Germans were busy binding up the wounds of war, making a living, building a roof over their heads. Gradually, however, with the slow return of prosperity through hard work and generous foreign support, the Germans found the physical energy and the psychological readiness to take a hard look at their past.

"Coming to grips with the past" is the term frequently applied to this process both in Germany and abroad. The Germans, humanly, are shocked and stirred by their growing comprehension of all that happened under the Hitler dictatorship. Both publicly and in private, they have felt shame about, and will certainly never forget, the tragedy that this regime visited on themselves and on other peoples. But as they look back, the same process also shows them what has happened to Germany since the overthrow of the Hitler dictatorship: New forms of dictatorship, imposed from outside, have closed down on two parts of the nation. For today only the Federal Republic is free. The Soviet Zone and the Eastern Territories are under Communist control.

There was a time when the average German, busy with reconstruction, was apt to say about the problem of his divided country: "It's terrible, but what can be done?" More recently, however, public-opinion polls and other evidences have indicated that the Germans now place reunification high on their list of priorities for the future. It can be assumed that, following the reunification of the Soviet Zone with the Federal Republic, the German people will look forward eagerly to their second item of unfinished business as a people: the negotiation of a peace treaty that will include the settlement (by negotiation, not dictation) of their eastern borders.

For the fact is that the German people cannot look back, as they have constantly been urged to do by their own leaders and by their friends and critics abroad, without seeing the *whole* past. They see both the tragedy of 1933-1945 and the second tragedy, from 1945 to the present. They are ready to make what atonement is possible for the tragedy caused by the Hitler dictatorship; but they cannot atone by giving away their own homeland.

Through the Eyes of the Traveler

It is not necessary to be German in order to experience the German-ness, the Western-ness of the civilization that since 1945 has been "annexed" by the East Bloc. At every hand the foreign observer in these areas can see the evidence himself. For example:

The town of Eger, with its beautiful medieval market square and the old town house connected with the name of Wallenstein. Eger was a city of the German Reich in 1277;

The Church of St. Mary in Danzig, one of the richest German monuments of religious architecture, with its magnificent Gothic madonna;

The Gothic town hall in Breslau, capital of Silesia. This building strikes the visitor as one of the most notable examples of Gothic secular architecture in Europe. It was erected in the 14th to the 16th centuries.

These are only three examples among dozens that link the Oder-Neisse area with the West. The visitor will find his own favorite examples at every hand. Predominant in the sphere of architecture are creations of Gothic art, many of them erected at about the time the cathedral of Notre Dame in Paris was nearing completion. The same spirit of creativity flowed from Lübeck past Rostock and Wismar on the Baltic through villages and towns, to Marienburg on the Nogat river and so onward in every direction.

Neither the river called the Oder nor the river called the western (or Görlitzer or Lausitzer) Neisse makes sense as a border. This river system goes right through half a dozen cities and a number of smaller towns. To these communities, the Oder-Neisse Line represents a partitioning that antedates by 16 years the wall the Communists built in August 1961 to partition the city of Berlin.

More accurately, the largest of these half-dozen cities, Stettin, would have been partitioned by the river — had not the line been bent at this point in Poland's favor. So today the old Hanseatic city, once world-known as Germany's biggest harbor on the Baltic, is called by its occupiers Szczecin. (But it remains Stettin, or at least Stettin/Szczecin, on maps of Europe that are printed in the free world. As we have seen, an international conference of geographers agreed after the war that the German placenames east of the Oder-Neisse Line are to be retained pending a peace settlement.)

Some 90 miles upstream is the old town of Küstrin. Its suburb of Kietz is on the west bank of the partitioning river and therefore is part of the Soviet Zone of Germany; across the river, the rest of the city, under Polish administration, is called Kostrzyń.

Perhaps none of the cities of the Oder-Neisse feels the effects of the arbitrary partitioning more than Frankfurt-on-the-Oder. In free western Germany, Frankfurt-on-the-Main has become one of the Federal Republic's most thriving and progressive cities. In unfree Frankfurt-on-the-Oder, however, life seems to have stagnated. The bridge across the Oder at this point leads from the Communist-controlled part of Germany to Communist-controlled Poland. The span was once part of a main artery between Berlin and Warsaw. Today the bridge is little used. For who travels nowadays from Germany's old capital to the capital of Poland? The Oder-Neisse Line not only separates cities and peoples; it isolates East from West.

Farther to the south the Oder bends toward the east; now the "border" cuts right through Brandenburg and then slices off the western tip of Silesia. It partitions the old provincial town of Guben. And it cuts through Görlitz; the German side remains Görlitz and the other side is known to the Poles today as Zgorzelec. Another of the partitioned communities is the town of Forst, 30 miles south of Guben. As for the town of Zittau, the Oder-Neisse Line left it intact — except for the soft-coal pits from which a large part of the community made its living. So runs, city by divided city and town by partitioned town, the line that the Communist propaganda calls "a peace frontier".

Why then this artificial frontier? It seems obvious that cities like Königsberg and Danzig, Stettin and Breslau, Liegnitz and Glogau, have the same kinship to Germany and free Europe as do their sister cities of equal rank and venerability in the West.

That this is no national myth, but is observable fact, can be witnessed by every traveller. Non-Germans have often expressed astonishment at finding so many architectural similarities in East and West Germany. Peasant houses in East Prussia, for instance, built in Saxon or Westphalian style; the magnificent churches and patrician houses in Danzig, Königsberg and Breslau — such are the tangible proofs of the kinship between the creative spirits of East und West.

"Who dares to draw a dividing line," asked Wolfgang Eschmann, "and say: Lübeck is German and so is Cologne; but Danzig, Königsberg and Breslau are something else? Who dares to say that the common growth of Europe that took place at that time will not suffice for the common aspirations of today?"

If this sentiment sounds more "European" than German, it is true that international attitudes have taken precedence over national concepts in postwar Germany. The whole history of free Germany's relations with the West since 1945 is one of trust and partnership. There would be no Oder-Neisse problem today if the German-Polish border could be negotiated by a free German people living in close economic, cultural and political kinship with

111

a free Polish people. But as things stand the temporary loss of the Eastern Territories is felt keenly as a double loss: a loss to Germany and a loss to freedom.

Part of a People's Past and Future

Here, in other words, is not a matter of a people's refusal to make atonement; the situation is, rather, that a people is simply unable to surrender a part of itself. The German Eastern Territories are part of the past which forms the German present and extends into the heritage of Germany's future generations. History, literature, nearly every subject taught in the German schools (and in many of the classrooms of the world) has some of its roots deep in the German lands of the East.

A humanist and internationally esteemed democrat, Former President Theodor Heuss, has said: "The history of the German mind, the German state and the German economy would be completely distorted, and fragmentary indeed, without the rich contribution which our nation in its entity has received from the Eastern Territories."

Both Prime Minister Churchill and President Roosevelt were astonished, and said so*, when they first heard the Stalinist line

* See the record of the American-British-Soviet conversation at Yalta, reprinted at the start of Chapter 5.

Nicolaus Copernicus, a Good European

Born in Thorn on February 19, 1473, died in Frauenburg on May 24, 1543. A true European to whom arbitrary national boundaries were as outdated as the idea that the sun moves around the earth, Copernicus studied at the University of Cracow, at Padua in Italy and later at Bologna. After settling at Frauenburg, Copernicus became increasingly dissatisfied with the Ptolemaic system of astronomy. There were men of like minds. Copernicus strove to rationalize divergent views. He contributed to Europe's history as to our knowledge of the universe.

Frauenburg

An idyllic view of the town of Frauenburg and its rustic surroundings.
The tower at the right is a memorial to Nicolaus Copernicus.

that Germany's Eastern Territories were historically Polish. This pretense served the Soviet endeavor to "compensate" Poland in the West for lands that the Soviet Government was preparing to take back from Poland in the East (Chapter 5). But the claim, as the American and British statesmen recognized, does not square with the facts of history.

Cultural Bonds Between East and West Germany

The truth is, as any objective geographer or historian can confirm, that the Oder-Neisse Line was drawn absolutely arbitrarily. Since 1945 it has cut through a cultural unity that had grown organically through many centuries. That is why the German people cannot simply "forget", even if they wished to do so.

When Duke Albrecht of Prussia founded the Albertus University in Königsberg in 1544, it stood from the beginning for a lively intellectual exchange between east and west, an exchange that the Iron Curtain makes impossible today.

From the Middle Ages until the present era, East German scholars have given their creative impulses to the free life of the West. Perhaps the greatest astronomer of all time, Nicolaus Copernicus, the father of our present picture of the earth and its place in the universe, was an East German.

So was the philosopher Immanuel Kant. His most famous dictum, even when expressed in the idiom of his day, continues to have a peculiar pertinence to the present-day problem of achieving fair play in central Europe:

> "Act only on that maxim whereby thou canst at the same time will that it should become a universal law."

The Eastern Territories were the native soil of other great names of the world of philosophy: among them, Johann Gottfried Herder, born in 1744 in Mohrungen; Arthur Schopenhauer, born in 1788 in Danzig ...

113

Among East German men of letters, outstanding as a representative of the classical period is the dramatist Heinrich von Kleist, born in 1777 in Frankfurt-on-the-Oder. From the romantic period came Josef von Eichendorff, born in 1788 in Silesia.

A carol sung at Christmas in many lands came originally from East Germany:

> "O du fröhliche, o du selige
> Gnadenbringende Weihnachtszeit,
> Welt ging verloren, Christ ward geboren,
> Freue Dich, freue Dich o Christenheit!"

The carol, created by Johannes Daniel Falk, came into existence in 1800 in Danzig.

The spiritual and intellectual flow from East Germany has continued unbroken from earlier into modern times. A few names will suffice as examples: Gustav Freytag, the 19th century novelist, dramatist and critic, born in 1816 in Kreuzberg in Silesia; Arno Holz, born in 1863 in Rastenburg, East Prussia; Hermann Sudermann, born in 1857 in Matziken, East Prussia; the well-known writer Gerhart Hauptmann, born in 1862 in Obersalzbrunn, Silesia; the West Prussian Max Halbe and another West Prussian, Hermann Löns, born in Kulm and known to the present day by nature-lovers as the poet of Lüneburg Heath.

It is on its face impossible simply to relinquish and forget about so living a part of Germany as that represented by the names. A memorial bust of Hermann Löns confronts a new generation of walkers, along a trail near Bonn, the provisional capital of the Federal Republic. Hauptmann's works have an international audience. Eichendorff is as much read and quoted by West Germans as he was by his countrymen in the East. And so one could proceed through the entire list ... A past that lives into Germany's present.

In the memory of many Germans alive today, Pomerania became a "border area" only after the Versailles Treaty (Chapter 4). Today it is under Polish administration. But its German-ness remains part of the Germans' living present. Cultural life in Germany and in the West generally owes much to many men of Pomerania. For example, there are the painter and wood-carver Bernd Notke, the reformer Johann Bugenhagen, the painter Caspar David Friedrich. There are the poets Ernst Moritz Arndt and Ewald Christian von Kleist; the physicians Theodor Billroth, Karl Ludwig Schleich and Rudolf Virchow. There are those pioneers among other pioneers of human flight, Otto Lilienthal and Hans Grade. There is the actor Heinrich George — and in the world of communications, the founder of the international postal association, Heinrich von Stephan.

Universities and Academies

Another bridge between East and West — until the Oder-Neisse Line of 1945 drew the Iron Curtain down across it — was the university life of East and West Germany. For centuries, German academic youth has followed the custom of dividing its student years between at least two universities, so as to gain a liberal education not only from textbooks but from a variety of teachers and a variety of landscapes. East German students tended to choose West and South German universities for a part of their studies, while West German students traditionally went East. The spiritual "cross-fertilization" that this exchange achieved has left its marks indelibly on today's Germany.

We have already mentioned the Albertus University in Königsberg, founded in 1544 with at least 80 professors and more than 130 other lecturers. In addition, East Germany gave Germany and Europe:

The Friedrich Wilhelm University in Breslau — created by merging the University of Frankfurt-on-the-Oder founded in 1506 with the Breslau University founded two centuries later;
the University of Greifswald, founded in 1456;
the State Academy in Braunsberg, founded in 1586;
and many other universities and academies founded at later dates in, for example, Danzig, Breslau and Königsberg.

Economic Ties With the East

Earlier in this chapter we considered the warning of an American delegation to an international conference about the economic harm done to Germany and Europe by the loss of the Eastern Territories. To illustrate the point, let us take a few figures at random from German official sources:

An important part of Germany's mineral and industrial resources was supplied by the Eastern Territories;

A considerable part of Germany's food supply came from these areas: for instance, 30 percent of the average potato crop, and about a fourth of the average sugar-beet production;

Nearly one-quarter of Germany's forests are behind the Oder-Neisse Line; and

One-fourth of Germany's traditional agricultural lands are in the Eastern Territories.

A Heritage of the Younger Generation

Against this social, political, economic and spiritual background, it is perhaps clear why Germans as a whole (not simply any particular group) consider a free and fair negotiation of the status of their Eastern Territories a matter of unfinished business.

National consciousness passes from generation to generation, like other concepts of humankind. So it has been with the Oder-Neisse problem. The elder statesmen of today's Germany bequeath it as

116

unfinished business to the citizens of tomorrow's Germany. For example, President Lübke recently recommended to German youth (1) the "indispensable effort to overcome the unnatural partitioning of our homeland" and (2) support for Europe's aspiration to weld its nation-states into "greater communities".* In countless such public utterances, German statesmen have foresworn the exaggerated nationalism of Europe's yesteryear — but have upheld the necessity of a reunited German homeland as a nucleus for international cooperation.

Not only respected elder statesmen like President Lübke (and former President Heuss, quoted earlier in this chapter) care about the future of the German Eastern Territories. Not only the young people, idealistic and groping toward a consciousness of themselves, their homeland and the world, care about it. The problem is growingly a concern of all ages and groups of the population.

Not only the expellees' organizations, but also the Federal Government of Germany and all parties in the parliament have repeatedly and unanimously declared that the German people can never simply forget about their Eastern Territories. This necessity of remembering and of achieving a settlement invariably is coupled with a pledge to seek recognition of German legal claims only through peaceful negotiations. Both in regard to the Soviet Zone of Germany and in regard to the Eastern Territories, the Germans have rejected any use of force in obtaining the restoration of the territorial integrity of Germany. But about the issue itself, German public opinion is well-nigh unanimous.

Looking to the Future: German Official Pronouncements

Earlier in this chapter we saw that from the beginning of its life the Federal Republic of Germany has made its intentions clear regarding the solution of the Oder-Neisse problem. In Chapter 6 we noted that Germany's allies in the free world — in particular France, Great Britain and the United States — have followed the

---

* In a message to the convention of university fraternities or "corporations" (Burschenschaften) in Berlin, January 3-5, 1962.

same policy. But the entire free world could hardly solve the German-Polish problem were the German people themselves to lose heart. Fortunately, the contrary has happened. German official statements on the subject have confirmed and strengthened the above-quoted pronouncement of 1950. Below are some of these official declarations of intention.

The German parliament (Bundestag) on December 5, 1952:

"Changes in the territory of the German state made in anticipation of the peace treaty are not recognized. They have no legal validity. The reunification of Germany may not be restricted to the reunification with the Federal Republic of the German territories on this side of the Oder-Neisse Line. In a peace treaty to be freely agreed upon, the German borders are to be fixed in such a way that they form the foundation for a lasting peace."

The Chancellor before parliament on October 20, 1953:

"In keeping with the numerous declarations of this parliament and of the Federal Government, the German people will never recognize the so-called Oder-Neisse Line."

The Foreign Minister on April 2, 1957:

"I am bound to declare, with the approval of the entire parliament, that the Federal German Government is not in a position, and no Federal German Government will be in a position, to voice a renunciation of the areas that have been taken away. On the contrary, we hope and wish that this question shall be cleared up in talks between a free Germany and a free Poland, in a way which will be to the benefit of both peoples and which will create the prerequisites for a good and friendly relationship between the two nations."

The Chancellor in September 1957:

"The Federal Government will uphold in the future as it has in the past the right of homeland and the right of self-determination.

118

The economic and social incorporation of expellees into the area of the Federal Republic does not impair the legal claim of homeland."

Undersecretary Carstens of the Foreign Office on October 11, 1960: *

"The German Eastern Territories within the German state borders of 1937 were not involved in or affected by the partitions of Poland at the turn of the 18th century. The German Eastern borders are among the oldest and most stable in the world's history. The German Polish border in Silesia has remained unchanged since the Treaty of Trentschin in 1335, and the German-Polish-Lithuanian border in East Prussia since the Peace of Melnosee in 1422 — in other words, since 157 or 70 years, respectively, before Columbus discovered America. Incidentally, the last census before the outbreak of the second World War showed that in the German East, in an area of 114,291 square kilometres, non-Germans totaled not more than 3.5 percent of the population."

Undersecretary Franz Thedieck ** *on October 29, 1960:*

"The Federal Government's legal standpoint and political conception in regard to the German Eastern Territories have been made public on many occasions. Let me summarize the position in seven statements:

"1. The Government of the Federal Republic of Germany is the only German government which has been freely and legally established; therefore it alone is entitled to represent the people in international affairs. The most basic and the principal goal of the Federal Government is and remains the restoration by peaceful means of Germany's unity as a state.

"2. In regard to the territorial state of Germany, the borders of the state as they existed on December 31, 1937, are determinant.

"3. The German people does not recognize the Oder-Neisse Line as the present or future border of Germany.

---

* In the Federal Government's "Bulletin" of that date.
** Of the Federal Ministry for All-German Affairs.

"4. The final determination of the borders of Germany is postponed pending a settlement reached in a freely agreed treaty of peace.

"5. Only an all-German government, a representation of the people that has been elected by the whole people, is authorized to confirm a decision on the future German borders in the East.

"6. The right of homeland and the right of self-determination are inevitable presuppositions for the solution of the German East problem.

"7. The solution is only conceivable by way of negotiation, which must take place without any threat or application of force."

Foreign Minister Gerhard Schröder on October 12, 1962:

"This free land works for the day when all Germany will again be free."

Chancellor Ludwig Erhard on October 18, 1963:

"It is our duty again and again to direct the attention of the world to the unresolved German problem ... For there should be no doubt that the German problem is one of the chief causes of tension in the world, and we cannot hope to remove these tensions if this problem remains unsolved ...

"We all fully realize that great difficulties must be overcome along the path towards the restoration of German unity . . . The Federal Government is convinced that at the end of this path there must be a peace treaty freely negotiated and concluded by a freely elected all-German Government. Such a treaty — and such a treaty alone — can, and must, determine the final frontiers of Germany, which, according to valid legal opinion, continues to exist within its frontiers of December 31, 1937."

120

Chapter 9:

BASES FOR SOLVING THE PROBLEM

"The present arrangement is not a German, not a Polish, not even a Russian solution; it is a Bolshevik solution. What we need is a European solution."

> Jakob Kaiser
> at the Deutsche Heimat im Osten, Exposition,
> November 1950

"Let us debate colonialism in full — and apply the principle of free choice and the practice of free plebiscites in every part of the globe."

> President Kennedy
> to the United Nations General Assembly,
> September 25, 1961

Politics, it has often been remarked, is the art of the possible. Politics is even more truly at the service of mankind, however, when it addresses itself to making possible what is desirable.

Is it possible to solve the Oder-Neisse problem in a "desirable" way — with a reasonable degree of consideration for the interests of Poland, of Germany, and of Europe? Is it possible, in other words, to achieve in central Europe the honorable international relationships that the United Nations seek to foster elsewhere in the world?

121

Twice within the memories of many of us, there have been world wars with their focal points in Europe. Today's Europe, in the wake of the two wars, is more tense, more sharply divided against itself, than Europe has been during any other time of peace in modern history. Indeed, today's arrangement between East and West in Europe is so far removed from a true peace than men call it a Cold War.

Moreover, the tensions in Europe today are in part the heritage of two postwar "settlements". The first settlement, the Treaty of Versailles of 1919, was meant to be permanent. The second, the Potsdam Agreement of 1945, was expressly declared to be temporary, and has yet to be replaced by a peace treaty. Both "settlements", the one of 1919 which did not endure, and the one of 1945 which was not meant to endure, go to the geographical heart of the tensions in central Europe today. Let us see what yesterday's "settlements" can teach us about a better foundation for peace in the Europe of tomorrow.

The Heritage of the First World War

Neither Polish nor German ambitions can be blamed for the outbreak of World War I — yet its settlement in the Treaty of Versailles created the basis for Polish-German tensions that have continued to the present day.

Historians have long known that the causes of the war of 1914—1918 were complex. Today informed persons agree that in plain truth there is no one nation which can be "blamed" for the first world war. If individual powers must be singled out at all, we find that two empires which no longer exist — the Russia of the Czars and the Austro-Hungarian Empire — figured most directly in the outbreak of World War I. Today it is a matter of open record that statesmen in London and Berlin, for example, tried until the last hour to avert the disaster. But tensions in the Balkans fostered tensions between two competing alliances; and war came.

As late as 1916, two years after the war broke out, there was not yet any general conviction among informed persons about war

122

"guilt". On the contrary, many American and European states-men were actively considering the prospects for a peace based on "no annexations and no indemnities". At a later stage of the war, the world was stirred by President Woodrow Wilson's idealistic "Fourteen Points".

Not idealism, however, but war-born emotions dominated the minds of European statesmen by the time the fighting finally ended in 1918. Woodrow Wilson's ideas were, to put it mildly, honored more in the breach than in the observance. The victors did not openly contradict the Wilsonian doctrine of self-determination in central Europe; they simply denied it, in large measure, to the Germans. (Chapter 3 records briefly the story of plebiscites held, plebiscites not held, and plebiscites held but ignored.)

The arbitrary territorial settlements of 1919 in central Europe — particularly as between Poland and Germany — sowed the seeds of future discord. President Wilson was among the first to see the danger. Early in April 1919 he commented: "The only real interest of France in Poland is in weakening Germany by giving Poland territory to which she has no right." *

The Polish-German settlement, more perhaps than any other single aspect of the Versailles Treaty, sowed the seeds of discord in central Europe. Soon afterward, in the West, farsighted French-men and Germans did their best to move toward rapprochement. Throughout the decade of the 1920s men like Aristide Briand for the French and Gustav Stresemann for the Germans tried to undo some of the injustices that were committed in the postwar fever of 1919. But time ran out. Hitler came to power.

To avoid misunderstanding, let the obvious be repeated here: No well-informed and fair-minded German considers the unfair treatment of Germany after World War I — an unfairness that has meanwhile been chronicled by a number of Allied historians — as an excuse for Hitler. On the contrary: the National Socialist dictatorship of 1933-45, far from "correcting the wrongs of Ver-

* R. S. Baker, "Woodrow Wilson and World Settlement", Vol. II, p. 60.

sailles", ended up inflicting new miseries of unparalleled magnitude on Germans and non-Germans alike.

Yet the unfortunate fact remains that Hitler was able to use the post-Versailles record of those territorial "adjustments" which were not based on self-determination. Before he took power, they provided him with a prime theme for his political oratory. Once he had taken power, he used the same record of Versailles to play on the emotions and paralyze the wills of both his German subjects and his neighbors in Europe.

Hitler remembered well, for example, that in the Allied nations there were many honest men who had agreed with Woodrow Wilson's analysis (see above) of the mistakes being made at Versailles; honest men who agreed, too, with Jan Smuts, the Prime Minister of the Union of South Africa, who on May 22, 1919, had written to Mr. Lloyd George, the British Prime Minister, that "the enlargement of Poland beyond anything which we had contemplated during the war" was an error "full of menace for the future peace of Europe".*

Moreover, Hitler knew how to take advantage of the uneasy consciences of Western statesmen. Shrewdly, the dictator placed first on his agenda for action the "correction" — in his totally unlawful and reprehensible way — of the more obvious wrongs of Versailles. He gambled on being tolerated by the West in his re-occupation of the Rhineland, and appeased by the West in his moves in other directions. By getting away with "correcting" one European situation after another by show of force, he strengthened his position. When there was no longer any stopping him short of bloodshed — whether from within Germany or from outside — Hitler launched his attack on Poland in 1939.

The "Settlement" After the Second World War

A glance at the maps in this book will show the German areas that were lost to Poland in 1919 — in a "settlement" that Woodrow

---

* Quoted by Rep. Reece, op. cit.

124

Wilson and others warned against. It will show, secondly, the additional territory that Germany would now lose to Poland, were she or her allies able to accept the Oder-Neisse Line as final.

Having lost important parts of their homeland in 1919 — when the urgings of prominent Allied statesmen failed to modify the terms of the Treaty of Versailles — the Germans are now being asked by the Communist Bloc to make further gifts to their Polish neighbor.

But it would be no contribution to world peace, under present Cold War relationship, if the Germans were to make such an unrequited concession to the Communist sphere of power. It is even highly questionable wheter such a transfer of territory would be legally possible, in any case, under existing conditions. For, ironically, the Communist policy that demands Germany's Eastern Territories for Communism is the self-same policy that rejects the concept of a German nation. Because of the present Communist efforts to block the reunification of Germany, there is literally no German government today legally authorized to sign away, in the name of all the Germans, the coveted slice of the German homeland!

It is true that if there were any German government that could theoretically make such a concession to the East Bloc, it would be the Federal Republic, with its provisional capital at Bonn, as the only freely elected German government. By contrast, the regime in the Soviet Zone of Germany (which went through the motions of handing over the Eastern Territories to Poland in the Görlitz Agreement of 1950 — Chapter 6 —) is so little authorized to speak even for its own subjects that it has had to erect a "death strip" through the countryside and a wall through Berlin to keep them from fleeing.

1919, 1945 and Today

Germany's concessions of territory to Poland after 1919 were valid under international law because an all-German government — acting under duress of hunger and defeat, it is true — signed a peace treaty of which those concessions to Poland were a part. In 1945, by contrast, the victors recognized that there was no German government to conclude a peace treaty. Accordingly, Poland and the U.S.S.R. were granted temporary administration of certain German areas pending a peace treaty to be negotiated with a government authorized to represent Germany as a whole.

Prerequisites for a True Settlement

(1) A Reunified Germany

Any lasting settlement of the Polish-German situation, therefore, must await, first of all, the formation of a government that represents the entire German people: those of today's Soviet Zone as well as those of the Federal Republic. Meanwhile, the Federal Republic has said repeatedly that, acting as trustee for the whole German people, it will insist that the question of Germany's eastern frontiers be kept open until a representative all-German government can negotiate them. In this stand, it has the backing of the Potsdam Agreement (of which the U.S.S.R. was a signatory) and the continued backing of its Western neighbors (see Chapter 8).

(2) A Polish Government Free to Negotiate

Even the Potsdam Agreement of 1945 which gave Poland the provisional right to administer German Eastern Territories was linked with a pledge that has not been kept: the formation of a democratic government representing the Polish people (Chapter 5).

Until Poles are free to talk openly with each other, it is hard to see how Poles and Germans can have conversations leading to long-range and mutually helpful settlements. Although there is hope that a more liberal state of affairs may one day be permitted in Poland, at this writing there is no such freedom of speech and opinion.

For example, The New York Times of February 14, 1962, carried the following report:*

---

* *New York Times,* international edition, in an article by Arthur J. Olsen.

126

WARSAW, Feb. 11 — A Warsaw discussion club, the only regular forum in the Communist world where speech has been free, has closed its doors. The management of the Krzywe Koło, the Crooked Circle, made the decision itself to shut down. Little choise was left to the directors of the private club, which counts many of Poland's most distinguished men among its 500 members. Communist party authorities gave the directors the option of suspending club activities voluntarily or of accepting an order to close down, according to reliable informants.

There have been occasional "thaws" in Poland since that report. And here an irony: It is admittedly true that a regime which the Polish regime pretends to believe is a German "state" and with which it maintains what it calls "diplomatic relations", the Soviet-occupied zone of Germany, is far less liberal, as Communist regimes go, than is present-day Poland. But neither the part of Germany that is behind the Iron Curtain, nor any other people behind the Iron Curtain, including the Polish, is yet permitted to do much about true reconciliation with the free Germans and with the West.

Grounds for Hope of a Change

While the partitioning of Germany and the lack of leeway that is presently permitted to the Polish people to conduct their own foreign relations have been obstacles to a German-Polish settlement, on the other hand there is reason at least to hope that both obstacles may be removed.

On February 23, 1962, as its contribution to an exchange of relatively cordial memoranda, the Federal Government of Germany reminded Moscow of the Soviet Government's own stand on the Germany problem:

1. On July 23, 1955, the Soviet Government agreed to a joint directive issued by the Allied governments of World War II, which stated: "The heads of government, recognizing their common responsibility for the settlement of the German question and the reunific-

ation of Germany, have agreed that the settlement of the German question and the reunification of Germany by means of free elections shall be carried out in conformity with the national interests of the German people and the interests of European security."

2. A Soviet aide-mémoire of March 19, 1958, declared: "In order to avoid further false rumors the Soviet Government deems it necessary to state anew that it advocates the conclusion of one single peace treaty with the whole of Germany." *

As for the second prerequisite, Polish freedom to conduct her own foreign affairs, no suggestion is here intended that the improvement of Polish relations with the West need constitute the slightest threat to Polish relationships with the Soviet Union. It seems obvious, however, that the interests of all concerned require that Poland should one day be permitted to negotiate an honorable arrangement with her neighbor Germany.

This goal is what Chancellor Adenauer had in mind when he noted that "Poland belongs to Europe, too." **

His successor, Ludwig Erhard, realizes, as did Konrad Adenauer, that much remains to be done before there can be a reconciliation of Poland or any other state behind the Iron Curtain with the rest of Europe. Said Chancellor Erhard in his Government Declaration of October 18, 1963: Bonn is prepared to examine with Warsaw and all other Eastern European capitals "step by step in what way on both sides any preconceived opinions can be eliminated and fears deprived of their foundation."

From the long-range view of Polish interests, the forcibly imposed Oder-Neisse arrangement (see Chapter 5) is part and parcel of a dictated way of life — in both domestic and foreign affairs — that Poland has endured since 1945. Now and then, despite the suppression, there are unmistakeable signs that the liberty-loving Poles, whatever ties of friendship they will retain with their powerful Soviet neighbor, will not accept dictation forever.

* Federal German Government memorandum of February 21, 1962, in reply to Soviet memorandum of December 27, 1961.
** *Tagesspiegel* (Berlin), October 23, 1953.

128

The Church of Mary in Danzig

Dates from 14th and 15th centuries. Is famed as example of German "brick Gothic". Views are of "Marienkirche" before and after World War II.

Stettin

Although Stettin on the Baltic is under Polish administration today, it is one of the most German — and one of the earliest to be German — of Europe's great cities. Next to Danzig, it is the second biggest German-settled port on the Baltic. Germans were there as early as the 12th century. It is dotted with medieval churches. Also famed is its 16th-century Renaissance palace. Photograph shows the "Hakenterrasse", with the museum (left) and the government building (right).

"Ferment in Poland" is the title of a recent *New York Times* editorial on this subject. It states:

> "While Germany has been calling for freedom and unity, a kindred echo has been heard at times even behind the Iron Curtain in Poland. For example, in the autumn of 1961, the Polish physicist Leopold Infeld 'demanded true freedom under Communist rule', as the *New York Times* reported. And economist Oscar Lange 'has called upon the Soviet comrades' to justify 'if they can' the inevitability of 'the Muscovite version of Marxism-Leninism'." *

Granted then that the common interests of all nations will foster the reunification of Germany and a peace settlement in central Europe. What specific steps are to be envisaged if we are to make possible a stable future relationship between the German and the Polish people?

A European Security System

No Pole and no German is so naive as to believe that the Polish-German problem can be solved by itself in isolation. On the contrary, both blocs of nations involved in the Cold War are so much affected by any potential change in the power relationships in Europe that a Polish-German settlement can come only as part of a general peace settlement.

Those who argue, however, that the Oder-Neisse problem will "solve itself in time" forget the history of nations. They forget the examples of Lorraine, of the Saar, of Poland partitioned and Poland free again. They misunderstand, too, the psychology of peoples: of men and women who have learned, through centuries of political evolution, to spend "millions for defense but not one cent for tribute" **; to conciliate but not to appease; to make voluntary

* *New York Times*, international edition, December 5, 1961.
** Charles Cotesworth Pinckney, when U. S. Minister to France, on a policy for dealing with the Barbary pirates, 1797.

sacrifices but not to accept dictation; to measure self-respect and freedom in the same scales with life itself.

"The German Government will never be able to recognize the Oder-Neisse Line", said as moderate and international-minded a statesman as Konrad Adenauer.* Then he added:

"Germany will, however, endeavor to settle the territorial question bound up there with a new spirit of peaceful international co-operation." There, in two consecutive sentences by a world-respected statesman, we have the difference between dictation and negotiation. There we have the case for a negotiated, rather than an arbitrary, border between a future Germany and a future Poland.

Polish-German Border Adjustments

A goal that two world wars failed to achieve — genuine re-laxation of tensions in central Europe — might well be fostered by a cool-headed process pursued in peace. What is proposed is some-thing new for that part of Europe: an objective, deliberate adjust-ment of the Polish-German frontier, in a process that would treat the two peoples who are involved as equal partners in an honor-able negotiation.

That may sound like a self-evident proposal. Yet, as we have been reminded in the beginning pages of this chapter, such a nego-tiation, without dictation or force on one side and resentment on the other, has not once taken place between Germany and Poland since 1918.

There is no need here to go into the various methods by which a border adjustment could be worked out. The world's statesmen know a number of ways, which have been tested in situations at least as difficult as the German-Polish situation.

* Eight-point memorandum to President Eisenhower of May 29, 1953. (From the *Bulletin* of the Press and Information Office of the Federal Government, July 31, 1953). For Chancellor Erhard's comparable stand, see p. 120.

Any approach to the problem is better than neglect of it until it festers and causes new tensions in Europe. There can be direct Polish-German negotiations (within the framework of a general European security arrangement, as mentioned above). Or there can be multi-national negotiations, with Poland and Germany partners to the deliberations.

Before negotiations even begin, there can be study of the problem by bipartite experts or by a multilateral commission. Experts, whether from Poland and Germany or from some neutral country on the other side of the globe, would find ample aspects of the Oder-Neisse situation on which to base their suggestions for improvement. They would find, for example, that the present border, entirely aside from its political and moral aspects, splits communities in two; places on one side of the provisional line cities that the World War II victors intended should be on the other side; reflects a wartime confusion between two rivers of the same name; partitions ethnic groups; complicates the problem of Europe's food supply; dislocates industries; constitutes a roadblock across some major trans-European traffic routes; and in general ignores the common-sense national needs of the peoples on both sides of the line.*

Any border settlement in central Europe will have to be a compromise. A *negotiated* compromise, however, will be far better preparation for a better tomorrow than was either the dictated arrangement of 1919 or the Communist-fostered and provisional arrangement of 1945. A negotiated border settlement will benefit both Poles and Germans.

* Some of the detailed criticisms of the Oder-Neiße Line as a boundary have appeared elsewhere in this volume. Critics have included Polish statesmen and military men; Germans of all political persuasions and from diverse areas of Germany; central European students of the problem. Britons including Sir Winston Churchill; Americans including Harry S. Truman and James F. Byrnes, and many others. These comments are available in most of the world's major libraries. The problem of a future boundary commission, in fact, would not be in finding things to improve but in selecting among the plentitude of suggestions that have been made — from persons of many nationalities — for improvement.

The Poles, Ukrainians and others now living in Germany's Eastern Territories will be able to sleep well of nights knowing that there is a duly ratified international sanction for the homes and lands they occupy. Moreover, Poles in general will breathe more freely, knowing that a deeply rooted cause of tension with their nearest Western neighbor has at last been removed. As an American legislator* put the situation to the U. S. House of Representatives:

> "When partitioned again in 1939, the people of Poland knew that the wrong perpetrated by Hitler and Stalin would not prevail, just as most of them instinctively know now that the wrong of their attempted annexation of the German provinces cannot prevail."

While putting Polish minds and consciences at rest, a negotiated settlement would also be acceptable to the present and future generations of Germans. Negotiations would mean that for the first time since 1918 the Germans would have a voice in the determination of their homeland's eastern frontiers. Any sacrifice that they would make voluntarily — in acknowledgment of the bitter past and as a contribution toward a better European future — would endure. A negotiated Polish-German arrangement would win psychological acceptance among Germans now living and yet unborn — a kind of acceptance that the two dictated settlements of earlier in this century could never receive.

It is needless to add that an arrangement that ended tensions between Poles and Germans, facing each other in Central Europe, would be of immense benefit to the world at large.

Beyond Border Settlements: International Liberalization

Nations that have reached the stage of being willing to discuss border negotiations are also at the stage of being ready to take other steps that will make their borders less important.

* Rep. Reece, op. cit.

There is still much talk, not all of it from Communist sources, about Germany's being "hated and feared" in eastern Europe. Is it Germany — or is it a bitter memory of a war committed by a dictatorship; a war that was as cruel to Germans as to the dictator's opponents? We can answer the question by referring to the post-1945 experience of Germany's wartime enemies in the West. Once upon a time France, for example, was called Germany's "traditional" foe. Again, as recently as 1949, at the time of the formation of the Federal German Republic, "anti-German" feeling was still so high in the Netherlands — another victim of Hitler's aggression — that German tourists were made, here and there, to feel less than welcome. All that has changed. What has altered the relationship of Germany and her Western neighbors in the past ten years? Let a recent communication from Bonn to Moscow* tell the story:

A "fundamental change... has taken place during the last decade in the mutual relations between the western nations...

"The economic unification of western Europe is not, of course, without influence on the mutual political relationships of the partner states. Not only the customs frontiers, but also the national frontiers are losing their importance.

"Today all the citizens of our (European Economic) Community can travel from one country to another without a visa and without even a passport.

"Naturally, there are open problems between the States of our Community, too. However, the mistrust, the nationalism and national antagonism which in past decades and centuries dominated policies between the Powers have been replaced in the new European Communities and in the Atlantic Alliance System by recognition of the fact that there are no longer any problems between the member States which cannot be solved in the spirit of justice and common interest."

* Bonn memorandum to Moscow of February 21, 1962; op. cit.

This example of international liberalization in Western Europe is proposed by many thoughtful persons as the key to Polish-German relationships in the Oder-Neisse areas. A border settlement could be accompanied by the guarantee of a number of freedoms to the affected populations on both sides of the Oder-Neisse Line and/or on both sides of the new, negotiated border. These freedoms could be guaranteed by a multinational treaty, and could be made part of the border settlement itself. The negotiators could agree that throughout defined areas of central Europe, whether nationally Polish or nationally German, certain basic measures of liberalization would apply to the local populations.

Freedom of Residence

Who is to stay in the Oder-Neisse lands after a future Polish-German settlement? The answer, as far as the Germans are concerned, is: Anybody who wishes to. Even the groups most directly affected by the Oder-Neisse arrangement of 1945, the expelled East Germans, in their Expellees' Charter of 1950, renounced any thought of retaliation. In proclaiming their own right to a homeland, the Germans could not in simple logic deny the right to others.

Let that point be crystal-clear: A Pole or a Ukrainian who has tilled the soil or held a factory job, and perhaps raised a family, in the Oder-Neisse area since 1945 has every human and moral right to remain. His right could be guaranteed by a treaty recognizing freedom of residence.

At the same time, freedom of residence involves the same freedom for former residents who were expelled; or their children; or other men and women of German or any other nationality who wished to go to the Oder-Neisse areas and earn a productive living.

Guarantees of freedom to stay and freedom to remain would not, fortunately, overtax the natural resources of the region. We have seen earlier, and will note again below, that there is room for many more millions of persons than are now residing in the Eastern Territories.

Finally, freedom of residence also involves freedom *not* to stay. Many Poles and Ukrainians might, on one individual ground or another, wish to move elsewhere: into the heart of Poland, for example; or westward, to Germany's Ruhr area in order to share in the prosperity there. Any person wishing to leave the Oder-Neisse area could receive financial and other help in taking up a new home and a new life elsewhere — east or west — in any country willing to grant him and his family an entrance visa.

Auxiliary Freedoms

International measures of liberalization in Germany's Eastern Territories would need to include a variety of subsidiary guarantees. In particular, national and ethnic groups would deserve and get full protection wherever they resided. In a community with a mixed Polish-German population (to take the most probable example of a mixture of ethnic groups), there would be schools using both the German and the Polish languages. Both languages would be recognized in public and commercial life. Persons of Polish, German, Ukrainian and any other ethnic roots would all be equal before the law. (Such things, it is true, are taken for granted in most communities of the Western world; but there has been such a history of tension in central Europe that it seems desirable to state the obvious ethnic and cultural guarantees here.)

Citizenship and Nationality

Residents of the internationally liberalized areas would have considerable leeway as to citizenship. If for a period of years some of the Polish-German areas are to be under international supervision (see below), a resident might retain during that period any nationality he possessed when taking up residence there. If instead of preliminary international administration of the Oder-Neisse areas, the territories are to become respectively Polish and German by immediate agreement, presumably those who choose to live in a given area would take up the nationality of the country to which

135

that area is assigned. Or, again, present residents might retain their present nationality, while being subject, of course, to the laws of the nation. Switzerland and Canada come immediately to mind as nations where citizenship does not conflict with differing ethnic roots and linguistic usages.

National or International Solution?

This chapter suggests a solution of the Polish-German problem by application of a combination of national and international measures. As for borders, national boundaries are suggested, because at this stage of the world's development it remains true that nationhood is the common basis of community life.

On the other hand, borders have lost a great deal of their significance in Western Europe because of the formation of international communities. The West Germans have been among the most willing partners in the new international arrangements. They have been quick to agree to any curtailment of national sovereignty — in areas ranging from tariffs to armament — that has been established by the international community.

Against this backgound, a reunified Germany, combining the present Federal Republic and the present Soviet Zone of Germany, would find it quite natural to agree to a similar combination of national and international arrangements with its eastern neighbors.

In the case of a Polish-German settlement, there might also need to be additional, specialized international control measures for an initial period of some years. The freedoms of residence and of movement and of ethnic culture that have been outlined above imply an immense amount of administration — for freedoms without executive agencies to apply them and courts to guarantee them are worthless. These administrative organs could be constituted according to standards embodied in the terms of Polish-German rapprochement. For example, joint Polish-German administrative machinery could be set up. Or the United Nations, or any agreed combination of "third-power" nations could be asked to provide administrative, judical and technical services in the areas in question. All of this has been done before in many areas of the world.

In close connection with the question "national or international solution?" is the question of timing. We have tried to show why time will not by itself solve the Oder-Neisse problem (see especially Chapter 8 in this connection). But once the elements of a Polish-German settlement are agreed upon, the timing of the implementation of the agreed measures is another matter.

The United States set a time for liberation of the Philippines and kept its promise. The French applied a gradual settlement to the Saar problem, resulting in the area's choosing to become German while at the same time yielding specified economic advantages for France. In the Polish-German areas of dispute, some persons have advocated the establishment of a condominium of the two immediately interested nations. Others have favored an international control at the outset, with plebiscites to be held at some future time. For the sake of remaining with one example, this chapter has stressed the possibility of a relatively early agreement on an adjustment of national borders.

No one approach, however, can be set forth as "the" key to the German-Polish problem. National or international control; timing of plebiscites, and all the related matters are proper subjects for negotiation. Whatever form of settlement is adopted as a result of negotiations, however, one thing seems obvious: The interests of several parties must be protected, and conflicts among them resolved by an orderly process. The most clearly interested parties in an Oder-Neisse settlement will be:

1. The German people, whose lands the areas were until the provisional settlement of 1945;

2. The Polish people, who have made use of these territories since 1945 and have acquired various interests there;

3. The present residents of the areas;

4. Returning residents and other future residents.

Resolving Conflicts of Interest

The conflicting national interests in the areas must be resolved by negotiations; and by some combination of the various other devices of temporary international control, timing, plebiscites, etc., that have been mentioned above. But what about the conflicts of interest at the individual level — the rival wishes and claims of (1) persons who lived in the Oder-Neisse areas before 1945 (2) persons who live there now and (3) persons who may choose to return there, or take up residence there for the first time?

It seems clear that "right of residence" cannot imply, in such a situation, a claim on a *specific* residence within the German Eastern Territories. Let us say a German farm family was expelled in 1945, and that a Ukrainian family has occupied the home and tilled the fields since that time. Provided both families claim the same farm and home, clearly an administrative or judicial decision must be made. Maximum protection must be afforded to both families. If it is decided that the Ukrainian family may stay on the land it has worked, the German family would have a claim on land and a home site (with the necessary aid, credits, etc.) of comparable value elsewhere. Conversely, if it were decided that the German family might re-enter the home and once more till the fields, then it would be necessary to follow a clearly defined procedure for compensating the Ukrainian family. The latter would certainly need to be compensated in cash, land, a home, credits, or any combination of these assets for the time and work it had invested in the German homestead since 1945.

Then too, what if a returning German family finds that its home is in ruins, the result of the war or of subsequent neglect? Surely this family deserves a new start elsewhere in the area. Or suppose a Polish family, observing the general process of resettlement, wishes to move elsewhere in the area; or to Poland; or to western Europe. Under our procedure this family, too, has a claim to assistance.

138

Conflicting individual claims, requests to take up new residences elsewhere, and the other personal and human demands that will arise in the Eastern Territories will obviously involve a small fortune in public assets: cash, credits, building materials, labor transportation. Who will pay?

The most common-sense answer seems to that in an area that becomes German again, the German government should pay. It would pay not only for the costs of individual settlements and resettlements, but it would also compensate the Polish government, over a period of years, for what the Polish people have invested in the region since 1945. The amounts involved in all this would, of course, be enormous. From the human standpoint, however, the money and credits would foster many productive lives and careers.

From the Polish national standpoint, the money (and for goods) received from Germany would be a substantial impetus toward attaining rationalization of agriculture, high levels of industry, and other national goals for the common welfare.

From the German national standpoint, the sacrifices involved would represent some degree of atonement for the crimes that were committed between 1939 and 1945 by a German dictatorship misusing the German name.

Who would pay in the areas that were to remain Polish, or perhaps to be assigned for a period to international control? In both these cases, too, there would be a substantial German contribution to the costs, the kind and amount of aid to be agreed by negotiation.

This discussion of "who should pay?" makes no pretense that there can be material atonement for all that happened in central Europe during the war and postwar years. It is tragically true that the dead of before and after 1945 cannot be restored to life; nor can the physical and spiritual scars of those who survived be healed with even the most generous grants of cash and subsidies. On the other hand, the very fact of a sincere effort at some degree of material atonement would be a substantial contribution to reconciliation in central Europe.

Human Settlements Not Impossible: Two Precedents Since 1945

Fair settlements that involve a multitude of individual claims, desires and needs, many of them conflicting, will be complicated. But, given good will, these settlements will be no more impossible than were two other vast settlements that have been undertaken by the people of the free part of Germany since 1949, the year when the Federal Republic was created in free elections.

One such settlement is the international field: the *Wiedergutmachung* or restitution program. In it, the Federal Republic of Germany (by contrast, incidentally, with the regime in the Soviet Zone of Germany) has undertaken to make compensation to victims of National Socialist persecution and their survivors. This program, too, has involved a multitude of persons, living and dead, their heirs, successors and relatives, in almost every country of the world. It has involved both documentation and cases where documentation was destroyed; both the testimony of witnesses and cases where no one survived who remembered. In brief, it has encountered almost every imaginable administrative and human difficulty. Yet the restitution program is being carried through, despite difficulties and delays, in a spirit that has won acknowledgment from spokesmen of the most numerous group of persecutees of the Hitler regime, the Jews.

The second program that sets a precedent for a solution of individual and group claims in the Eastern Territories is the Federal Republic's domestic program of *Lastenausgleich or "equalization of burdens"*. What is to happen after a war in a multitude of unequal human situations such as these two: (1) a bomb has destroyed a man's house while (2) the home of the man's neighbor has happened to come through intact? Impossible as it may seem, the free German people have taken on their shoulders the job of providing material compensation to level out, as far as possible, inequalities of this kind.

The degree of success of these immensely complex programs gives hope of similar programs in the German Eastern Territories — programs to benefit Poles, Ukrainians, Germans and others, not on a basis of nationality but on a basis of need.

No Further Expulsions; Enough Room for All

Communist propaganda has pretended that the German people have in mind an expulsion of the Poles and Ukrainians from the Oder-Neisse territories, as most of the Germans were expelled from the area in 1945. It bears repeating that this idea is of corse absurd. Not only would a second injustice piled upon a first be no service to the Polish-German rapprochement that the Germans seek, but also, to turn from political and moral to social and economic considerations, there is room in the Oder-Neisse area for all who wish to earn a fruitful living there.

Even in the years before 1945, the population density of the regions was such that it could have supported many more than the 10 to 12 million Germans who lived there. Today, about 6 500 000 Poles, Ukrainians, etc., are settled there. The population does not begin to exploit the natural resources; and, it is, moreover, a population that has not been able to grow despite the application by the Polish government of an energetic resettlement policy.

If one bears in mind this situation alone — that 16 million persons certainly can make a living in the Oder-Neisse territories under present conditions, while in fact only 6 500 000 are there — then there is every practical possibility of an arrangement by which Poles and Germans could live together peaceably in these areas; as in fact Germans and Poles have done through most of their history.

141

Building on Centuries of "Peaceful Co-Existence"

To state that Poles and Germans and other central and East European folk have lived together peaceably throughout most of their history is simply to state facts. There have certainly been shortsighted political actions, such as the various partitions of Poland, in the times before the concept of democratic self-determination was common currency. There have also been shortsighted violations of self-determination, in the settlements after 1919 that ignored plebiscites (see Chapter 4) and in the provisional settlement of 1945 based on mass expulsions. But these long-past and recent events, however sensational, have been the exception. We have seen that for many centuries the Polish-German border was one of the most stable in Europe. More than that, the peoples themselves lived together without incessant thought of national rivalries and national boundaries.

It is historical fact that "peaceful co-existence" was a reality among the so-called "common people" of central Europe long before the Cold War elevated the concept of "peaceful coexistence" to a matter of world politics.

If one cares to look far back for signs of a German-Polish spiritual accommodation, they are plentiful as early as the 13th century. For one example, Duke Heinrich IV of Breslau, from the Slavic princely family known as the Piasten, became a celebrated German Minnesinger.

If one prefers to look to more recent times, the very names of the people of central Europe are proof of "peaceful co-existence". The countless living individuals with German first names and Slavic family names, and vice versa, are, to put the case mildly, a sign that there is no unsurmountable aversion between the two peoples!

Needed: Positive Acts of Reconciliation

The spirit in which any of the efforts at Polish-German settlement are undertaken can make or break them. With a desire for rapprochement, the Poles and Germans can do much to achieve a mutually advantageous reconciliation.

For one example, the study of history in both German and Polish schools can well afford to depart from the narrow nationalism that has characterized much of it in the past. It is not necessary to sacrifice objective treatment of past conflicts, but at the same time the many past and potential forces for friendly co-existence can be emphasized: such events as the reconciliation accomplished by Otto III and the Saxon kings of Poland, for example; the German influence on certain spheres of Polish religious life; the welcome extended in Germany to the Polish freedom fighters of 1831 and 1848.

In the sphere of the arts, teachers and cultural leaders in both lands can draw attention to the mutual attraction of German and Polish culture, as reflected, for example, in the works of Conradus Celtis and Stanisław Przybyszewski. There can be recognition in the East of German and other West European contributions to the architecture and municipal planning of much of Poland; and at the same time, there can be fuller recognition in the West — for example, in the German universities, some of which are, in fact, already taking steps in this desirable direction — of the importance of Slavic studies.

A Start Can Be Made

In Germany, and as soon as possible in Poland, there can be forums where free Poles and free Germans can get together. As intelligent men, they can seek not to win immediate agreement on all questions but rather to realize that they have common rather than separate problems. At the German universities where *Ostforschung* — study of Eastern Europe — is carried on, Polish social scientists and comparable scholars from other countries, can be invited to work on problems of relations between national and ethnic groups. Such steps may sound academic. But in actuality they would be a move toward something immensely practical for the future of central Europe: inter-ethnic cooperation as a replacement for the inter-ethnic rivalry that has been fostered by two world wars and their settlements.

Chapter 10:

AN ISSUE THAT CONCERNS THE WORLD

"Let us start to apply the conception that European matters which are of general concern should be dealt with in the general interest... We must avoid making a settlement which would only create difficulties for Poland and for Europe in future years."

> U. S. Secretary of State George C. Marshall at Moscow Conference of Foreign Ministers, 1947

"Annexation is the violation of a nation's right of self-determination."

> Lenin, Collected Works, Vol. 19, p. 304

"I would only say to our Polish friends that as, last time, they made a mistake in going too far East, so this time, I fear, they are making a mistake in insisting on going too far West."

> Anthony Eden, British Foreign Minister, to the House of Commons, August 20, 1945

"Poland has neither the human nor the material means of digesting the German territory up to the Oder River. These territories are a gift fraught with danger."

Władysław Anders, Polish general,
December 14, 1946

"The same people who now urge the Poles to accept the Russian offer will blame them in the future for having created, through their imperialism, a new problem which will trouble the peace of Europe."

Oskar Halecki, Polish historian,
April 1945

"If peace is to be permanent it must before all things be a peace of peoples."

Sir Bernard Pares, British historian
(1867 — 1949)

"The Communists ... are trying ... to interpose barbed wire, bayonets and tanks against the forces of history."

U. S. President Lyndon B. Johnson,
then Vice President, in Berlin,
August 20, 1961

Why should the peoples of the world concern themselves about a line drawn through central Europe? Because the Oder-Neisse Line is the tangible symbol of one of the main sources of tension between East and West.

A farsighted Polish general warned (see above) that the Oder-Neisse arrangement was not good for Poland. Nor is it good for

Germany, nor for Europe — and clearly what endangers Europe is a danger to the world.

Then why was the Oder-Neisse Line drawn?

One answer is that, long before the second world war was over, Stalin's plans for central and eastern Europe began to take shape; and the provisional Polish-German relationship that perplexes the world today was a basic element in those plans. The Stalinist tacticians of 1945 believed that a westward expansion of Poland at the expense of Germany would

1. Amount to a geographical extension westward of the Communist empire, represented in Poland by a Communist puppet government; and

2. Keep German-Polish relations in a state of tension — thus providing the conditions of unrest in Europe that Communist planners of Stalin's day welcomed.

And why, this being so, were the Communist plans not opposed by the Western participants of the war? To a considerable degree, they were. But sheer might, personified by the Red Army, prevailed over right at that time in eastern and central Europe.

Not, however, without protests from the free world — protests that remain today as our best guides to the underlying causes of the unsatisfactory situation in central Europe. At that time, the free world's sympathies naturally were with the aspirations of the Polish people for freedom after the years of Hitler's aggression. Even so, long before peace had come, and long before there was the free, democratic government that exists in Western Germany today, Western statesmen saw trouble ahead. They foresaw that no good could come of the postwar settlements if Poland were to absorb vast new reaches of German territory in addition to those she was awarded after World War I.

146

An incident at Yalta in February 1945 is worth repeating in this connection. Documents of that U. S.-British-Soviet conference tell a revealing story.*

At the conference Mr. Molotov, the then Soviet Foreign Minister, was busy advancing Stalin's plans for a westward expansion of Poland — a Poland that, as events were to reveal, was to be under control of Soviet Communism. Discussing provisional borders, Molotov suggested "the return to Poland of her ancient frontiers in East Prussia and on the Oder".

President Roosevelt asked how long it had been since these lands were Polish.

Mr. Molotov replied: very long ago, but they had once been Polish**.

Said the U. S. President, laughing, to Prime Minister Churchill: "Perhaps you would want us back?"

And the British Prime Minister replied: "Well, you might be as indigestible for us as it might be for the Poles if they took too much German territory."

Despite these clear misgivings of the leading statesmen of the free world, however, the Red Army and Communist pressure prevailed. The areas in question went to Poland — *but only provisionally, pending a peace treaty.* This fair negotiation of the Polish-German problem in connection with a peace treaty is still being awaited by the German people.

Unfinished Business

Unfortunately, a negotiated Polish-German settlement is still part of Europe's unfinished business. True, the Communist Bloc has now

---

 * Source is given at start of Chapter 5.
** Actually, the Germans had had possession of the area uninterruptedly since 1335 (Silesia) and 1422 (East Prussia) — since long before the discovery of America by Columbus. See Chapter 3; also Undersecretary Thedieck's summation, Chapter 8.

and again pretended that the matter was settled once and for all in 1945. However, the East Bloc's sporadic appeals to this or that nation to "recognize" the Oder-Neisse Line as being the Polish-German border betray the Communists; they know that this line is not and cannot be the final settlement.

Indeed, the Western Allies, although unable to stop the push of Communism through eastern Europe in the chaotic year of 1945, took pains to make sure the Polish-German matter would be left open for later settlement. This is the testimony of one of the conferees at Potsdam on the matter:

"To remove an excuse for Poland or the Soviet Union to claim that the line had been established or that there was any promise to support a particular line, the Potsdam Protocol declared: The three heads of government reaffirmed their opinion that the final delimitation of the western frontiers of Poland should await a peace settlement. In the light of this history, it is difficult to credit with good faith any person who asserts that Poland's western boundary was fixed by the Conferees."*

The Effect on Europe

Meanwhile, not the Germans, but the Americans, have provided what is perhaps the best statement of the importance of the Oder-Neisse problem to Europe — and therefore its importance to the world. Moreover, that statement was provided shortly after the second World War, when passions aroused by war and by the atrocities of the Nazi dictatorship were still fresh.

It was at the Moscow Conference of Foreign Ministers held between March 10 and April 24, 1947, that the U. S. delegation, led by Secretary of State George C. Marshall, spoke lucidly about the importance to world peace of a fair settlement in Central Europe. The American position taken at that conference has re-

* Former U. S. Secretary of State James F. Byrnes, "Speaking Frankly", p. 81.

mained a guideline of U. S. policy ever since; and it is also a fair reflection of the attitudes that have been expressed more than once by statesmen representing other nations of the free world.

Here are highlights of the American attitude as expressed in Moscow:

A fair settlement of the Polish-German frontier problem is in the general interest. "We are dealing with the problem that touches closely on the political stability and economic health of much of Europe ... We should see to it that the new frontiers ... do not create a continuing problem and are not barriers to the accustomed and healthful flow of trade and commerce and human intercourse."

Although Poland should receive territory and industrial resources "capable of maintaining her people at a good standard of life", *Poland should only be awarded areas which she "needs and can effectively settle"*. (Compare with the statement by the Polish General Władysław Anders quoted above and in Chapter 6: "Poland has neither the human nor the material means of digesting the German territory up to the Oder River.")

"We must avoid making a settlement which would only create difficulties for Poland and for Europe in future years."

Germany should not be deprived of one-fifth of her prewar food supply. (Compare with, for example, the difficulties that were to arise in 1961-1962, when problems of Germany's food supply, as reflected partly in agricultural prices, were an important factor in the negotiations of the European Economic Community over the Common Market's entry into its "second phase" of integration.)

For economic reasons, "there is danger in requiring an eventual German population of over 66 000 000* to live within the confines of a smaller Germany".

* This "eventual" figure of 66,000,000 was foreseen in 1947. By 1962, the actual population of the two parts of Germany not counting the Eastern Territories had reached more than 73,000,000.

A solution should be fair so as not to "discredit the democratic forces in Germany".

A solution should keep alive the possibility of *genuinely peaceful and cooperative* Polish-German relations in the future.*

Along the same lines, U. S. Secretary of State Marshall at the subsequent Conference of Foreign Ministers in London said: "*We must bear in mind that much of the territory now under Polish administration has long been German*" and added that it contained resources "*of vital importance to the German and European economy*".**

The Issue: Negotiations — or Dictation Once More?

The issue we are considering is broader than a matter of rival Polish and German claims. It is broader even than a matter of tensions in the geographical heart of Europe. The Oder-Neisse question has world-wide application. It is this: Are international relations to be based upon negotiation by the peoples involved or to be based on dictation? Two world wars in our time remind us that we can hardly afford further dictated settlements, with all the resentments and new tensions that follow in their train.

At this writing, the peoples affected cannot negotiate, for part of Germany is unfree and Poland is unfree to conduct her own foreign relations. But the day will surely come when the two neighbors in central Europe, together or in concert with other nations, will be permitted to work out their common future.

As the late President Kennedy put the case, the problem is a matter of applying the same fair standards to European peoples that we are beginning to apply to the peoples of Africa and Asia:

"Let us debate colonialism in full — and apply the principles of free choice and the practice of free plebiscites in every part of

* U. S. Department of State Bulletin, April 20, 1947, pp. 693—694.
** Documents on American Foreign Relations, Vol. IX, p. 45.

the globe."* The U.S. President also asked whether the Soviets were prepared to accept "in Berlin — and indeed in Europe — self-determination, which they profess in other parts of the world."**

When such a liberalization comes to central Europe, there can be negotiations. Meanwhile, the Polish Communist regime, which was aided and abetted originally by the Stalinist policies of the war years, wishes the world to believe that a fait accompli exists. Warsaw — under Communists who take policy instructions from Moscow — insists that Germany's Eastern Territories became part of Poland when the Poles were permitted to occupy these areas in 1945.

What do non-Poles (and non-Germans) think? National concerns aside, what is the international-law status of the East German areas?

A Soviet View: No Annexations

The Communist regime in Poland, as said above, argues that Germany's Eastern Territories became part of Poland in 1945. (The regime's own inner doubts on the point are reflected, however, in the constant "demands" it makes for world recognition of the action.)

For good reason, from its standpoint, the regime in Warsaw would like very much to be able to clothe its actions in Eastern Germany with a show of legality and permanence. For, as it stands, the Warsaw claim to final possession of East German areas is at variance with Moscow's own oft-stated views on self-determination. Lenin's succinct point against annexations is quoted at the start of this chapter. And when the Second All-Russian Congress was going about the business of shaping a state, it championed a doctrine that makes entire sense in connection with today's Oder-Neisse problem. The Congress called for plebiscites to be held "with abso-

* Source cited at start of Chapter 9.
** At the President's news conference, Washington, June 28, 1961.

lute freedom of all inhabitants of the said areas, including emigrants and refugees".*

Two recognized Soviet international-law textbooks, by Durdenevski-Krylov and by Korovin, reject the concept of annexation. Says the latter: "The Socialist State — the Union of Soviet Socialist Republics — is a voluntary union of peoples who aspire to no territorial conquests and reject the annexation of territories against the will of the people thereof."**

A Belgian View: Occupation, Not Annexation

Ernest Nys, an eminent Belgian jurist, an Associate Justice of the Hague Permanent Court of Arbitration, has stated:

> "The right of conquest is a thing of the past. Annexation of territory and transfer of sovereignty no longer take place as the invading army advances; a more equitable idea has been imposed in the form of military occupation.***

This legal interpretation takes on added significance when compared with a similar attitude apparently held by the Polish Prime Minister Sikorski. As noted in Chapter 5, he took with him to Washington, D. C., in December 1942 two memoranda outlining Polish ideas about postwar settlements. They did not mention annexation (cf. the Belgian jurist above: "... a thing of the past"). Instead they proposed a *military occupation* of German areas after the war, and drew the analogy of French occupation of the Rhineland after the first world war.

---

* "Declaration of Rights of the Peoples of Russia", adopted by the Congress of November 15, 1917.
** Quoted by Rep. Reece, op. cit.
*** American Journal of International Law, 1911, Vol. 5, p. 84.

152

A British View: "No Matter How Great the Need —"

A British international lawyer, Coleman Phillipson, puts the matter comprehensively as follows:

> "Encroachment on a nation's territory is not sanctioned by international law. International law, for its entire edifice, has been built up on the assumption of the autonomy and independence of sovereign states... No matter how great a particular nation's need of additional territory may be, it cannot justify the seizure of another nation's land.*

The Briton's phrase "no matter how great a particular nation's need..." may be compared with the Polish "need" for the Oder-Neisse areas. See, for example, the Polish general's candid statement, quoted above, that Poland lacked the means to "digest" the German Eastern Territories; and Sir Winston Churchill's famous remark at the Yalta Conference: "It would be a pity to stuff the Polish goose so full of German food that it got indigestion.**

A French View: No Denationalization as a Punishment

It has been noted (Chapter 1) that the Hague Rules of Land Warfare of 1907 — as well as Article 48 of the 1949 Geneva Agreement (also signed by the U.S.S.R.) — take stand against mass expulsions of population — like those expulsions which Stalin in early 1945 falsely assured his Western Allies had become a fait accompli in the Oder-Neisse areas. (See Chapter 5.)

Years earlier, a resolution of the *Institut de Droit International* of September 20, 1896, stated:

> "Denationalization can never be imposed as a punishment.***

* "Termination of War and Treaties of Peace", London, 1916, p. 29 ff.
** Quoted at start of Chapter 6.
*** Annuaire d'Institut de Droit International, Vol. XV, p. 271.

In other words, the Oder-Neisse settlement involving the expulsion of millions from their ancestral homelands, cannot have the quality of a final settlement on grounds that it was justified as a "collective punishment" of the citizens of Germany, for Hitler's war or for the dictatorship's atrocities. The French jurists' view on the point was confirmed in our own time by a verdict of the International Court at Nuremberg against Hermann Göring:

> "One of the most important legal principles consists of the individual character of criminal responsibility, and mass punishment should be avoided."*

An American View: "The Usage of the World —"

The respected pioneering Chief Justice John Marshall of the United States has pointed out that under international law only a treaty of peace can establish transfers of territory. His words:

> "The usage of the world is, if a nation be not entirely subdued, to consider the holding of conquered territory as a mere military occupation until its fate shall be determined at the treaty of peace.**

What is the gist of the various statements of international law above? In the Oder-Neisse situation, they add up to this concept: Polish presence on German soil can only be provisional pending agreement on the matter in a peace treaty.*** That was precisely the position taken by the victorious Allies — the U. S. S. R., the United States and Great Britain (France associated herself with the for-

---

* "The Trials of Major War Criminals", Vol. I, p. 256.
** U. S. Supreme Court, American Insurance Co. v. 356 Bales of Cotton (1 Pet. 511), 1828.
*** "Polish presence" refers here to international-law concepts. Poles, Ukrainians, etc., now living in the disputed areas may, as far as the Germans are concerned, remain there after a settlement. See Chapter 9 for a summary of the German desire to follow a policy of "live and let live" in the Eastern Territories.

154

mula soon afterward) — in the Potsdam Agreement of 1945.
(Chapter 5).

The Western Allies and the Problem

The international-law concept that we have sketched above,
quoting jurists of many nations, has been given "teeth" by Allied
policy since 1945. The New York Conference of the Western Foreign Ministers of Sept. 28, 1955, stated in a communiqué:

> "... the foreign ministers reaffirm the repeatedly expressed
> position of their governments that a final determination of
> the frontier of Germany must await a peace settlement for
> the whole of Germany."

Earlier, on October 4, 1954, Germany's major Western allies
made the same point: that only a peace treaty can determine
Germany's boundaries and that the Federal Republic, as the only
free and legitimately constituted German government, is recognized
as spokesman for the German people pending formation of an all-
German government*.

16 European Nations and the Problem

Meanwhile, too, the Council of Europe, representing 16 nations,
has put on record its conviction that the Germany problem is
"bound up with a wider European problem". The Council's Con-
sultative Assembly:

> Favors Western negotiation with the Soviet Government
> "on the German problem as a whole";

* London Conference of that date.

155

Urges the Western powers to "take all steps likely to lead to a settlement enabling the peoples of Central and Eastern Europe . . . to exercise their right of self-determination".*

When Are Boundaries "Sacrosanct"?

An American legislator** has pointed out that a venerable European tradition has been to respect national boundaries, even when it has been necessary to overthrow a national ruler who had overweening ambitions. He notes that "Napoleonic France . . . had overrun Europe, had partitioned and dismembered nations, had brought untold misery to millions of people, until she was finally crushed. Yet the victorious European allies at the Vienna Congress left France within her pre-Napoleonic boundaries***, with her territory undisputed, including Alsace-Lorraine."

He also asks why a sort of double standard should be applied to Germany — one in the West, another in the East. He says:

> "It seems somewhat incongruous that the German boundary toward Belgium and France should be regarded as sacrosanct, while the German-Polish boundary, going back many hundreds of years and surely equally sacrosanct, should be subjected by some people to a sort of seesaw game."

This chapter has suggested some of the reasons of economics, politics, historical precedent, international law and common sense why the Oder-Neisse Line concerns many thoughtful statesmen in many countries. Perhaps the most important aspect of the German-Polish problem, however, is that it sharpens the intensity of

---

* Resolution adopted in Strasbourg on September 25, 1961. Reported in *The Bulletin* of the Federal German Press and Information Office, October 3, 1961.
** Rep. Reece, op. cit.
*** Cf. the German wish to retain Germany's national boundaries of 1937, as they existed before Hitler started his conquests.

the Cold War. It is true that the German-Polish problem did not begin with the Oder-Neisse settlement of 1945. In modern times, it began with the setting of East German boundaries after the first world war. The Versailles Treaty was a dictated treaty, as historians have long since conceded.

The Oder-Neisse settlement, which at least provisionally takes away from Germany still a larger slice of her Eastern Territories than did the Treaty of Versailles, thus becomes the second border settlement of this century in which the German people have no voice. Some of the Germans are willing to make any sacrifice to atone for the second world war *except* the sacrifice of something they feel they have no right to sign away: parts of their ancestral homeland. (See Chapter 8.) Most Germans are willing in principle even to make substantial territorial concessions (as stated in Chapter 1). But they ask to do so — this time — as a result of negotiations in which they take part.

Dictated Borders Pile Up Trouble for Future Generations

The difference between a dictated settlement and a negotiated settlement is psychologically enormous. A dictated settlement that is accepted by one generation may become a national shame in the minds and feelings of the next. France kept alive the memory of her lost Lorraine for many decades, between 1871 and the outbreak of the first world war. In times past, the Irish made of their frustrated wish for homeland a bitter and bloody saga, known around the world. Poland kept alive her consciousness of nationhood throughout the times of her partitions — and who can say but that the excessive Polish territorial demands chronicled in this book* were not in a sense emotional compensations for the decades when Poland was not free?

Although Germans have solemnly and repeatedly foresworn the use of force in attempting an adjustment of their Eastern Territories

* See Allied und Polish warnings to Polish nationalists; Chapters 5, 6, 7.

problem, the mere existence of the tense situation hinders a normal and peaceful development for Europe.

"The Seeds of Future War"

An American news magazine recently described in blunt terms the ultimate danger in central Europe:

> "It has been argued that the West should give official recognition to what is presently a fact of geographical life: the Oder-Neisse Line...
>
> "This would perpetuate what West Germans now call the 'Three Germanys'* . . . But in any such three-way dismemberment of Germany lie the seeds of future war..."**

This book has concentrated on only one phase of the central European problems that came in the wake of World War II. Besides the Polish-German question, another question raised by the Potsdam Agreement of 1945 was its award to the Soviet Union — again, pending confirmation in a peace treaty — of the old German city of Königsberg and adjacent areas. Mention of the Königsberg arrangement has been restricted to a single footnote in this book.***

Besides the Oder-Neisse and Königsberg situations, there are of course other pieces of unfinished business in central Europe — "unfinished business" in the sense that these situations still await acceptance, or reconsideration, by the peoples involved. But there is no problem in central Europe that could not be solved in a spirit of international negotiation — as comparable problems have been or are being solved in western Europe.

---

* Referring to (a) the Federal Republic of Germany, (b) the Soviet Zone of Germany and (c) the Polish- and Soviet-occupied German Eastern Territories.
** *Time*, October 20, 1961: "The Real German Question", pp. 19—20.
*** In Chapter 1.

To concentrate on the Polish-German situation is not to deny the existence of the other problems — ethnic, political, economic, territorial — in central Europe. For several reasons, however, the Polish-German piece of unfinished business represented by the Oder-Neisse situation is the most important single aspect of the central European agenda that awaits settlement in a general peace agreement. In sheer size — square miles and millions of persons involved — the Oder-Neisse areas are many times greater than, for example, the Königsberg region that was provisionally assigned at Potsdam to the U. S. S. R. Again, geographically the Oder-Neisse areas are very nearly in the heart of the divided continent. Finally, the Oder-Neisse Line as a border separating East from West is rivalled in significance only by the equally artificial border that presently divides West Germany from Central Germany.

In any case, this book is only superficially about a line that has been drawn provisionally across the map of Europe. These pages also reflect the problem of the whole Iron Curtain, of which the Oder-Neisse Line is a major segment, yet only a segment. Our discussion concerns the problems of bringing back together peoples who historically have lived and worked together. It concerns the possibility of bringing to central Europe some of the gains in mutual trust and common welfare that have marked the progress of Western Europe since World War II.

Although some solutions and some bases for solutions of the German-Polish situation have been suggested (Chapter 9), only a few of these specific steps can be undertaken at present by men and women of good will. The other steps must be the decision of peoples and governments. A cornerstone of the whole hoped-for improvement will be the conclusion of a peace treaty with a reunited Germany, within the framework of a broad European agreement, protecting the security and promoting the welfare of every people of Europe.

Nevertheless, our particular subject of survey here has its own, immediate, world-wide significance. The Poles and the Germans, neighbors for centuries, partners in the construction of Europe, are major participants in the central European political drama today. If Poles and Germans can take even small first steps toward reconciliation, Europe will be taking steps toward reconciliation with Europe.

And it goes almost without saying that a new relationship between East and West in Europe would brighten immensely the prospects of better international relationships throughout a long-suffering yet ever-hopeful world of nations and neighbors.

Gerhart Hauptmann

lives on in German memories — as in the memories of persons everywhere who love literature. A younger generation of Germans is growing up familiar with his works and with his Silesian — that is to say, East German — background. What it would have meant to him had he been expelled from his beloved Silesia (the train that was ready to transport him was ready when he died on June 6, 1946) is perhaps indicated by his last words: "Am I still at home?" Born in 1862, Hauptmann in his long lifetime gave the world a small library of humanist writings. He was a friend of prominent men of letters in Britain and America.

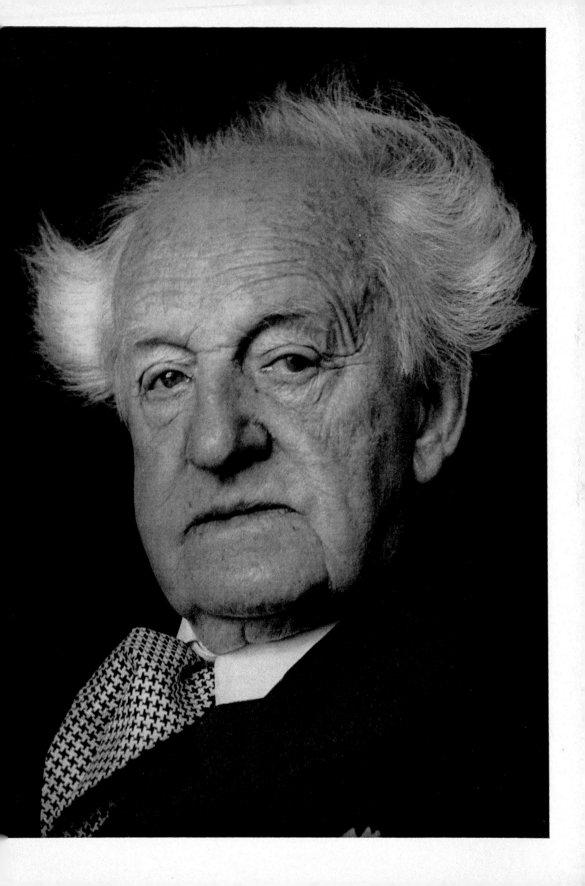

Breslau

As early as the 13th century there was a German settlement in Breslau. After being conquered by the Mongols, the city was liberated and rebuilt. In 1261 it obtained the Magdeburg charter of civic rights and became the capital of the province of Silesia. Before World War II, Breslau had some 630 000 inhabitants. Today, under Polish administration, the city is called "Wrocław". The picture shows the city hall on the so-called "Ring".

Appendix:

CHARTER OF THE GERMAN EXPELLEES

On August 5, 1950, this "Charter of the German Expellees"
was proclaimed by the unknown expellee in Stuttgart at
a large rally in the presence of members of the Federal
Government, of the Churches and of the Parliaments. The
Charter bears the signatures of the elected spokesmen of the
various fellowships (Landsmannschaften) and of the
chairmen of the Central Union of German Expellees and
its Land Unions. It was endorsed at large rallies in all
parts of Germany.

Conscious of their responsibility before God and men,
conscious of their adherence to the Christian community of the
Occident,
conscious of their German origin, and realizing the common task
of all the nations of Europe,

the elected representatives of millions of expellees, having carefully
deliberated and searched their conscience, have resolved to make
public a Solemn Declaration to the German people and to the entire
world, in which are defined both the duties and the rights which
the German expellees consider their basic law, and an absolutely
indispensable condition for the establishment of a free and united
Europe.

161

1. We, the expellees, renounce all thought of revenge and retaliation. Our resolution is a solemn and sacred one, in memory of the infinite suffering brought upon mankind, particularly during the past decade.

2. We shall support with all our strength every endeavor directed towards the establishment of a united Europe, in which the nations may live in freedom from fear and coercion.

3. We shall contribute, by hard and indefatigable work, to the reconstruction of Germany and Europe.

We have lost our homeland. The homeless are strangers on the face of the earth. Almighty God himself placed men in their native land. To separate a man from his native land by force means to kill his soul.

We have suffered and experienced this fate.

We, therefore, feel competent to demand that the right to our native land be recognized and be realized, as one of the basic rights of man, granted to him by the grace of God. We do not, however, wish to stand aside and be doomed to inactivity, as long as this right is not realized, but want, rather to strive and toil with every member of our nation in a new spirit of community life, in a manner purified by a spirit of brotherly consideration. For this reason, we claim and demand, today as in the past:

1. Equal rights as citizens, not merely before the law, but also in the hard realities of every day's life.

2. Just and reasonable repartition of the burdens of the last war among the entire German people, and an honest execution of this principle.

3. A sensible integration of all professional groups of expellees into the life of the German people.

162

4. An active part of the German expellees in the reconstruction of Europe.

The nations of the world shall be conscious of their share of the responsibility for the fate of the expellees, who have suffered more than all others from the hardship of our times. The nations shall act according to their Christian duty and conscience.

The nations must realize that the fate of the German expellees, just as that of all refugees, is a world problem, the solution of which calls for the highest sense of moral responsibility and the stern necessity of making a tremendous effort.

We, therefore, call upon all nations and men of good will to join in the mutual task of finding a way out of guilt, misfortune, suffering, poverty and misery, which will lead us all to a better future.

Stuttgart, August 5, 1950.

Dr. Linus Kather
Member of the Bundestag
Chairman of the Central Union
of German Expellees (ZvD)

Josef Walter
Chairman of the Union
of Expellees in Land Hesse

Helmut Gossing
Chairman of the Union
of Expellees in Land Lower
Saxony affiliated to the ZvD

Dr. Mocker
Chairman of the Land Union
of German Expellees, Wurttemberg

H. Eschenbach
Land Union of German
Expellees, Stuttgart

Wilhelm Zeisberger
New Citizens' League, Bavaria

Dr. Alfred Gille
Chairman of the Union
of Expellees in Land Sleswig Holstein

Dr. Bernhard Geisler
Chairman of the Union
of Expellees from the East
in Land North-Rhine-Westphalia

Erwin Engelbrecht
Chairman of the Union
of Expellees in Land Bavaria
affiliated to the ZvD

A. Deichmann
Chairman of the Land Union
of German Expellees,
Rhineland-Palatinate

Roman Herlinger
Main Committee of Refugees
and Expellees in Bavaria

Dr. Rudolf Lodgman
von Auen
elected spokesman of the
Sudeten Germans' fellowship

Erwin Tittes
elected spokesman of the
Transsylvania Germans'
fellowship in Germany

Dr .Rudolf Wagner
elected spokesman of the
Bukovina German Resettlers' fellowship

Dr. Alfred Rojek
Chairman of the Union
of Expellees in Land Berlin

Walter von Keudell
elected spokesman of the
Berlin-Brandenburg fellowship

Dr. Konrad Winkler
Chairman of the League
of Expellees, South Baden

Axel de Vries
elected spokesman of the
German-Baltic fellowship

Franz Hamm
Chairman of the
Yugoslav Germans' fellowship

Erich Luft
Union of Expellees in Land
Bavaria affiliated to the ZvD

Dr. Bartunek
Land Union of German Expellees,
North Baden

Dr. Schreiber
elected spokesman
of the East Prussian fellowship

Erik von Witzleben
elected spokesman
of the West Prussian fellowship

Dr. Walter Rinke
elected spokesman
of the Silesian fellowship

Anton Birkner
elected spokesman of the
Carpathian German fellowship Slovakia

v. Bismarck
elected spokesman
of the Pomeranian fellowship

Waldemar Kraft
elected spokesman
of the Vistula/Warthe fellowship

Dr. Gottlieb Leibbrandt
elected spokesman of the
Resettlers from the East cooperation
(Germans from Russia)

Dr. Kimme
Chairman of the Union
of German Expellees in Land Bremen

Dr. Kautzor
Chairman of the Union
of Expellees in Land Wurttemberg
Hohenzollern and Lindau